Sinatra

A PORTRAIT OF THE ARTIST

Sinatra

A PORTRAIT OF THE ARTIST

RAY COLEMAN

Foreword by Bono of U2

Turner Publishing, Inc.

ATLANTA

For my brother, Maurice Coleman

Also by Ray Coleman

LENNON: The Definitive Biography of John Lennon

McCARTNEY: Yesterday And Today

THE CARPENTERS: The Authorised Biography

CLAPTON: The Authorised Biography of Eric Clapton

STONE ALONE: The Definitive Story of the Rolling Stones
Co-written with Bill Wyman

ROD STEWART: The Biography

BRIAN EPSTEIN: The Man Who Made The Beatles

I'LL NEVER WALK ALONE
Co-written with Gerry Marsden

Published by Turner Publishing, Inc.
A Subsidiary of Turner Broadcasting, Inc.
1050 Techwood Drive, N.W.
Atlanta, Georgia 30318

Library of Congress Cataloging-in-Publication Data

Coleman, Ray.
    Sinatra: portrait of the artist/by Ray Coleman.—1st ed.
        p.   cm.
    ISBN 1-57036-213-0 (alk. paper)
        1. Sinatra, Frank, 1915– . 2. Singers—United States—Biography.
1. Title.
ML420.S565C65 1995
782.42164' 092—dc20
[B]   95-19970
                                                                        CIP

Distributed by Andews and McMeel
A Universal Press Syndicate Company
4900 Main Street
Kansas City, Missouri 64112

10 9 8 7 6 5 4 3 2 1

First published in Great Britain in 1995 by Pavilion Books Limited

Designed by the Bridgewater Book Company
Picture research by Juliet Brightmore

Printed and bound in Singapore

CONTENTS

You Know His Story Because It's Your Story

im still starstruck, it doesn't wear off... frank sinatra gave me a solid gold cartier pasha watch with sapphires and an inscription... to bono with thanks FRANCIS A SINATRA... WATER RESISTANT... im not gonna get over this... Frank likes me... hell ive hung out with him, drunk at his bar, eaten at his table, watched a movie at his place... in his own screening room... dig that asshole... i usually drink j.d. straight up without ice, its a tennessee sipping whiskey, so why did i go and blow it by ordering ginger ale... "jack and ginger" a "girls drink"... FRANK looks at me and my two earrings and for the first time in my life i felt effeminate...i drank quickly to compensate and worse i mixed my drinks... over dinner (mexican not italian) we drank tequila in huge fishbowl glasses, never drink anything bigger than your head i thought as FRANK pushed his nose up against the glass like it was a hall of mirrors...

later asleep on the snowwhite of FRANK and BARBARA'S screening room sofa I had a real fright i woke up to wetness, a damp sensation between my legs... hmm... dreams of dean martin gave way to panic... first thought: ive pissed myself. second: don't tell anyone. third: dont move theyll see the stain... yellow on white. fourth: make a plan... and so i sat in my shame for twenty minutes, mute waiting for the movie to end, wondering as to how i would explain this... this... irish defeat to italy... this sign that what was once just verbal incontinence has matured... and grown to conclusive proof that i didn't belong there/here. i am a jerk. i am a tourist, i am back in my cot aged 4... before i knew how to fail—mama— ive pissed myself... again.

well i hadnt, id spilt my drink. i was drunk, high on him, a shrinking shadow boxing dwarf following in his footsteps... badly... STARSTRUCK... "what now my love? now that its over?" i went back to the hotel... (turn left on frank sinatra boulevard). i would never drink in the company of the great man again... i would never be asked to. wrong, twice.

NOTE: IF YOU'RE GONNA DROP ONE, DROP A BIG ONE... A NAME... A NAME TO HANG ON YOUR WALL. EPISODE NO.1. *december 93, u2 had just got back from* TOKYO, *the capitol of zoo tv, it was all over... I felt wonderful. I felt like shit. my* TV *had been turned off... it was christmas... there was a parcel from* FRANK *a large parcel... i opened it.... a* PAINTING, *a painting by* FRANK SINATRA *and a note... "you mentioned the jazz vibes in this piece well its called* JAZZ *and we'd like you to have it. yours Frank and Barbara" this is getting silly... there is a* SANTA CLAUS *and hes Italian... (opera, Fellini, food, wine, Positano, the sexy end of religion, football, now grace and generosity?)... heroes are supposed to let you down... but here i am blown away by this 78-year-old saloon singer and his royal family... starstruck... a skunk on the outskirts of las vegas with my very own Frank Sinatra, last seen in his very own living room, on the edge of his very own desert, in palm springs...* THE PAINTING, *a luminous piece as complex as its title, as its author... circles closed yet interlocking, like glass stains on a beermat... circles with the diameter of a horn... Miles Davis... Buddy Rich... rhythm... the desert... theyre all in there... on yellow... to keep it mad... fly yourself to the moon!*

EPISODE NO. 2. MARCH 1. *im not an alcoholic im irish, i dont drink to get drunk do i? i drink because i like the taste dont i? so why am i drunk? im drunk because Frank has just fixed me another stiffy thats why! jack daniels this time straight up and in a pint glass.*

its the "Grammys" and ive been asked to present the boss of bosses with a life achievement award... a speech... i know im not match fit but of course i say yes.

and now im in NEW YORK CITY *and so nervous i am deaf and cannot speak... two choices;* BLUFF *or concentrate on the job at hand, i do both and end up with a rambling wordy tribute with no fullstops or commas... that might explain how I felt about the man who invented pop music... and puncture the schmaltz... a little...*

anyway we're in FS's dressing room (the manager's suite) where the small talk is never small, im talking to Susan Reynolds, Franks p.a. and patron saint and Ali (my wife and mine). Paul McGuiness (U2's manager) asks Frank about the pin on his lapel... "its the legion of honor... highest civilian award... given by the president..." which one? enquires paul... "oh i dont know... some old guy... i think it was lincoln..." cool... do you have to be american to get one? i think to myself... already feeling my legs go...

next up the award for best alternative album u2 are nominated for this... better get ready... whats the point... we're never gonna win that... that belongs to the smashing pumpkins one of the few noisy bands to transcend the turgid old-fashioned format theyve chosen... you have to go downstairs... you might win... whats there to be embarrassed about... youve been no.1 on alternative/college radio for 10 years now... its the most important thing to you... tell them... its your job to use your position... abuse it even... tell them... you're not mainstream you're slipstream... tell them... you'll make it more fun... that you'll try to be better than the last lot... tell them you're mainstream but not of it and that you'll do your best to fuck it up... TELL THEM YOU KNOW FRANK... tell the children... so i did.

The speechifying below wasn't heard in the uk so loud is the word fuck over there but Frank heard it and Frank liked it... so here it is:

Frank never did like rock 'n' roll. And he's not crazy about guys wearing earrings either, but hey, he doesn't hold it against me and anyway, the feeling's not mutual.

rock 'n' roll people love Frank Sinatra because Frank Sinatra has got what we want... swagger and ATTITUDE... HE'S BIG ON ATTITUDE... SERIOUS ATTITUDE... BAD ATTITUDE... Franks THE CHAIRMAN OF THE BAD.

rock 'n' roll plays at being tough, but this guy's... well, he's the boss of bosses. The Man. The Big Bang of Pop. I'M NOT GONNA MESS WITH HIM; ARE YOU?

who is this guy that every swingin city in america wants to claim as their own? this painter who lives in the desert, this first-rate first-take actor, this singer who makes other men poets, boxing clever with every word, talking like america... Fast... straight up...

"ive hung out with him, drunk at his bar... he may be putty in Barbara's hands but im not gonna mess with him are you?" Bono on left with Frank at the bar.

in headlines... comin' thru with the big schtick, the aside, the quiet compliment... good cop/bad cop in the same breath.

you know his story because it's your story... Frank walks like America, COCKSURE*...*

Its 1945... the US cavalry are trying to get out of Europe, but they never really do. They are part of another kind of invasion. A.F.R. American Forces Radio, broadcasting a music that will curl the stiff upper lip of England and the rest of the world paving the way for Rock 'N' Roll—with jazz, Duke Ellington, the big band, Tommy Dorsey, and right out in front, FRANK SINATRA*... his voice tight as a fist, opening at the end of a bar not on the beat, over it... playing with it, splitting it... like a jazz man, like miles davis... turning on the right phrase in the right song, which is where he lives, where he lets go, and where he reveals himself... his songs are his home and he lets you in... but you know... to sing like that, you gotta have lost a couple o' fights... to know tenderness and romance like that... you have to have had your heart broken.*

people say Frank hasn't talked to the press... they want to know how he is, whats on his mind... but y'know, Sinatra is out there more nights than most punk bands... selling his story through the songs, telling and articulate in the choice of those songs... private thoughts on a public address system... generous... this is the conundrum of frank sinatra left and right brain hardly talking, boxer and painter, actor and singer, lover and father... troubleshooter and troublemaker, bandman and loner, the champ who would rather show you his scars than his medals... he may be putty in barbaras hands but i'm not gonna mess with him are you?

LADIES AND GENTLEMEN, ARE YOU READY TO WELCOME A MAN HEAVIER THAN THE EMPIRE STATE, MORE CONNECTED THAN THE TWIN TOWERS, AS RECOGNIZABLE AS THE STATUE OF LIBERTY... AND LIVING PROOF THAT GOD IS A CATHOLIC... *will you welcome* THE KING OF NEW YORK CITY... FRANCIS... ALBERT... SINATRA.

love + pizza
Bono

Growing old, declared that authority on the subject, Groucho Marx, was what happened to you if you were lucky. And Somerset Maugham wrote that aging was better than the alternative.

Such aphorisms seem to sit comfortably atop Frank Sinatra because, at the age of eighty, he destroys time itself. When people in their twenties are stirred by his music, caring not a jot whether he is forty or ninety, the proof is final that the sound of Sinatra is immortal. For millions he is the way we were, the way we still are, the way we will always want his certain style of music to be.

Yet to discuss and absorb Sinatra's work, it is essential to step beyond the territory of music alone, for he is much more than a pivotally important vocalist; a strong image of the man is embedded in the mind of anyone who has experienced his passing show in the past six decades.

He's the hip swinger with the tilted fedora, tie casually askew as he stands in the recording studio close up to the microphone; he's the wounded lover and the man who found marital bliss eventually. He's the pugnacious guy taking no prisoners in the 1960s, revelling in well-documented episodes of irascibility with the press. He's the out-of-luck singer who, well and truly on the ropes, had us cheering when he made the most amazing comeback in the history of entertainment. He's the gifted actor in pictures as diverse as *From Here to Eternity* and *High Society*; the dedicated philanthropist devoting huge amounts of his energy, money and spirit to world charities. He's the much-vaunted leader of the hedonistic Clan. He's the record company boss and talented business strategist; the champion of many a troubled friend in show business; the close ally of US presidents; the doting father of three who said he wished he had more children.

Doing It His Way

All these images of the man, and others, coalesce. Whether you admire Frank Sinatra is irrelevant to the fact that through the weight of his personality he has towered over the entertainment world like a colossus; and his place in history ensures that he will continue to do so, long beyond this, his eightieth year.

While he is famous for being the perennial king of cool, it is as a singer of popular songs that Sinatra will always be primarily revered. To think of Sinatra is to think of "Witchcraft" and "Come Fly with Me," of "My Way" and "I Get a Kick Out of You"; of "Stardust" and "Misty" and "It Might as Well be Spring" and "The Song is You." As the chief custodian of the timeless compositions of Richard Rodgers and Lorenz Hart, George and Ira Gershwin, Cole Porter and Sammy Cahn and Jimmy Van Heusen, Frank Sinatra stands as the most innovative interpreter of popular song in this century. He is, moreover, utterly irreplaceable: who else will run the gamut of styles, from "Here's That Rainy Day" through to "New York, New York," with his unassailable authority? Only imitators.

He is no saint and his public behavior has often been condemned quite justly. But the prodigious quality and quantity of his records and live performances dwarf any of the negative incidents that have marked his life. A glance at the discography by John Ridgway, and the filmography by George Perry, at the rear of this book offers proof if needed that Sinatra should be judged by his contribution to art and entertainment rather than by his notoriety, by which the media and others have often pigeon-holed him.

Taking songs from the pens of lyricists and composers of enormous stature, Sinatra presented them as masterpieces of modern art; he was and is an innovator because, while others before and after him were perfectly capable of singing a good song, Sinatra, from his earliest days, vowed to sing differently.

The key to his genius lies in the degree to which he has invested himself in his work. Sinatra never merely sang the notes, but added his own emotive interpretations of the human condition to his singing. It is no surprise that he has named Tony Bennett, a similarly creative soul with a unique stamp, as the best singer in the world. To Sinatra, exerting oneself is what makes an artist, makes a song come alive.

With swagger, panache, mastery of phrasing, vocal timbre, Sinatra gripped his own generation and remains very much in vogue.

It follows that the actual quality, and density, of his voice, becomes inconsequential with the passing of the years. Few people, surely, listened to his music and remarked: "What a great VOICE up there!" Rather, we valued him for the special nuance and phraseology he brought to great songs, the swagger, panache, and ability to infuse something of his own multifaceted personality into the work of lyricists that he usually chose carefully and tastefully.

Sinatra gripped his own generation and, uniquely for an artist dispensing popular music that is marked by fads and fashion, he is still very much in vogue. He has achieved his stature because of his age, and not in spite of it, and the commentaries on his "gravelly voice" and his "inability to sustain notes" are completely beside the point. Sinatra in 1995 must be celebrated as a living legend, that corniest of phrases that might have been invented for the likes of him.

His mastery of phrasing, his vocal timbre, and his special emphasis on consonants in a style of enunciation that he alone has created… these spring lightly from him, bearing down on us like old friends; familiar and welcome, and the best to savor because they are a little wrinkled.

This book is a portrait of the artist and of the man who invented that artist: Frank Sinatra. In the 1950s, when he broke through on record with the million-selling single "Young at Heart," I was a teenager, only vaguely aware of his name from a scratchy, crimson-labelled Capitol 78 rpm of "Nancy (With the Laughing Face)." There was a wink in his voice, a *knowingness*, that was like nothing I had heard. Forty years on, the effect of Sinatra with those two songs is clearly etched in my memory. I had been a Bing Crosby and Al Jolson devotee (and still am); yet the magic, the difference, the sheer conviction carried by the Sinatra voice was strangely affecting. Hitherto, one's expectations of a baritone were that he should render a strong lyric and good melody with a purity of style. The songs did a great deal of their work. In the early 1950s, Perry Como, Nat King Cole, Eddie Fisher, Al Martino and Guy Mitchell were fine artists, but they scarcely applied muscle to their vocals.

Frank Sinatra came with an attitude as well as a voice, and he set his own agenda. He was going to be a great big star by his own definition; that became clear as he was laced with Nelson Riddle in the 1950s to begin a partnership as crucial to that decade as was that of John Lennon and Paul McCartney to the 1960s.

Since those heady years of songs like "Swingin' Down the Lane" and "Love is Here to Stay," the man has been consistent and the artist has grown immeasurably. And, above all else, it is as a singer nonpareil that he takes his place in the pantheon of show business. The imagery of Sinatra will be with us forever: swinging songs from the hip; the swirl of cigarette smoke and his lone figure picked out by a single pink spotlight; a glass of Jack Daniel's in his hand, literally or figuratively.

In a bar off Lower Broadway in New York City hangs a sign: "It's Mister Sinatra's world. We just live in it." The singer himself, a grand master of hyperbole in and out of his public life, would surely adore that epithet. For all our yesterdays, todays and tomorrows in popular song, the towering presence of Sinatra will never be out of style, because he is style. This book aims to celebrate just that.

Ray Coleman
Cornwall, England

*Feeling
So
Young*

"Leave your ego at the door." The intimidating advice from the record producer was firm, as a stream of distinguished contemporary singers arrived at his studio over a two-month period.

If he really needed to reproach the artists about their attitude to the sessions, an even more resonant message was coming from the heavyweight record chief: "History is being made here."

And even in the heady world of show business, so accustomed to hyperbole, this was no exaggeration. Frank Sinatra was about to reclaim his dormant crown as the hippest singer on earth. And a gold-carat selection of the world's hottest "newer" singers was going to ensure that he achieved just that. They were going to duet with him on some of his best-known songs.

**Opposite: Sinatra's
style was hip from
the beginning.**

It was July 1993. At the age of a seventy-seven, the legendary figure of Sinatra had no real need to prove anything. He was indeed established as the most compelling solo artist in popular music. And yet, while history had established him as timeless, Sinatra had often displayed an almost uncanny ability to be timely, too. Staying contemporary had always been a crucial part of Sinatra's make-up and it was to come into play with devastating effect. In recent years, some had bemoaned the fact that his voice was not what it was, that perhaps he should retire with dignity, his reputation secure. But his fifty-year journey from Hoboken, New Jersey, to Hollywood, California, had never been marked by timidity.

And the people who gathered around Sinatra to recreate his quintessential songs were as hip to current trends as they were reverential to Sinatra's stature. Phil Ramone had an immaculate pedigree as a record producer for such artists as Paul Simon, Billy Joel, Barbra Streisand, Gloria Estefan, Dionne Warwick and many more. Co-producer Hank Cattaneo has produced such epic shows as "Barbra Streisand in Central Park" and the "Beatles at Shea Stadium." And yet the return of Sinatra to the Capitol Records Studio A in Hollywood, where he cut his teeth on so many memorable tracks back in the 1950s, created an excitement and tension in even the most hardened professionals.

In 1990 he embarked on a diamond jubilee world tour, starting with his 75th birthday celebration at Byrne Arena in New Jersey.

In February 1993, at their first meetings with Sinatra to moot his return to the recording studio, two of the key men who would help make it happen met Sinatra's most frequent question: "WHY?" Ramone and Don Rubin, EMI Records' executive vice-president for artists and repertoire, had gone to see him in California with two ideas for the singer. One was for a live album, to be recorded perhaps at New York's Rainbow Room with an array of the world's best musicians. The second suggestion was more unorthodox for Sinatra: an album of duets with other artists. Characteristically, Sinatra responded strongly and positively. "He was over the moon with excitement at the idea of the duets," Rubin recalls. "There was no apprehensiveness. He realized, also, that to return to the studio and do what he had done for the last forty years was not intriguing."

Sinatra's speedy decision had to be matched. "He is not a patient guy," Ramone smiles. "He wants to know: 'You're doing it, you're not doing it/we're recording/we're not recording?' You can't have another agenda. He tests the water all the time."

The project moved rapidly. Ramone and others drew up a list from which Sinatra approved the singers who would be invited to duet with him. The contrast in artistry was as startling as the idea itself: from Charles Aznavour to Bono of U2, from Tony Bennett to Luther Vandross, from Carly Simon to Julio Iglesias, from Anita Baker to Kenny G, and on to Liza Minnelli, Barbra Streisand, Aretha Franklin, Gloria Estefan and Natalie Cole.

The setting was chilling, historic. In 1956, Sinatra had been the first to record in Studio A of what would become the legendary Capitol Records Tower in Hollywood. Now, in June 1993, he was back, soberly suited, to confront a dozen songs instantly identified with him. No duettists were present. Their voices were to be added to Frank's recorded vocals later, in a slice of modern technology that would astonish anyone of Sinatra's vintage. From recording studios around the world, the duettists with whom Sinatra was teaming up awaited word that the sessions had gone successfully and that their input was to be digitally inserted.

This technique bewildered and displeased many observers. One major rock star, initially eager to participate, rejected the invitation when he learned that the duets would not actually be "live" in the studio. He had wanted the eyeball-to-eyeball experience of working with Sinatra, rather than producing a "phantom" duet. Many Sinatra fans, too, balked at the fact that the duettists had not been in the studio with Frank. "Technology duetting" was about to have its finest hour, however: the project steamed ahead, with artists eager to help recreate music with a giant. There was incredulity, too, at his wish to push himself into such a daring operation at this stage of his life. What, many wondered, did Frank Sinatra need to prove?

"Why would I want to do these songs again? Are they going to be *better?*" Sinatra asked Phil Ramone when they entered the studio. Feisty even at this late hour, Sinatra questioned even his own wisdom in an aside to Phil Ramone. Well accustomed to soothing the famous with reason and logic, Ramone replied: "The truth is that you will sing these songs *differently* now from how you did fifty years ago. And I want to hear that difference. Your maturity, your angst, is different from when the vocal cords were just producing pretty sounds." Noting that Sinatra was a perfectionist, Ramone says now: "He's the actor's actor, and the singer's singer, and he's a guy you have to answer properly with the truth. I said to him that *Songs for Swingin' Lovers* had not been done with modern technology: reinterpretation of some of his finest songs at his age was something for generations to experience."

Sinatra is hardly the kind of man anyone would challenge, but this telepathic communication seemed to touch a nerve with him. On the concert trail around the world, Sinatra was doing a hundred shows a year, not the most likely routine for a seventy-seven-year-old. This, alone, signalled his love of making music, his biological need to carry on. And Ramone had spotted it.

With his pianist of forty-two years, Bill Miller, and a fifty-two-piece orchestra under the baton of Patrick Williams, Sinatra set to work. It was not all plain sailing. Customarily, a singer goes into a booth and, with headphones, sings while physically isolated from the musicians. That enables the production team to get a good separation of sound that can later be mixed perfectly. Sinatra quickly rejected this in favor of his habit of many years, positioning himself amid the orchestra so he could feel the music, respond to it, as their voice. Not every session was successful. "He refers to his voice as 'the reed,'" Ramone says. "He would say: 'The reed's not happening tonight, fellas. See you tomorrow night.'"

The vocal equipment was not, of course, the major issue here. His power is inevitably reduced. But what remains intact, what can never leave Sinatra, is his style. The phrasing is unique, as creative, as deliberate and mesmerizing, as ever. And he stamped that imprimatur right across the album that would become *Duets,* released on 25 October 1993.

Here he was, strutting with Liza Minnelli on "I've Got the World on a String," which Nelson Riddle's punchy arrangement had helped redefine as Sinatra's craft on the *Songs for Swinging Lovers* album in 1956. Here was Frank with old friend Tony Bennett on the quintessential Sinatra rendering of the film theme, "New York, New York," one of his many signature songs. With Julio Iglesias on the brooding "Summer Wind"; with Aretha Franklin on the dramatic "What Now My Love"; with Natalie Cole on a swinging "They Can't Take That Away from Me"; with Barbra Streisand on an exquisite reworking of his oldie, "I've Got a Crush on You"; with Luther Vandross on the old Sinatra warhorse "The Lady is a Tramp."

Pulling Sinatra abrasively into the 1990s, Bono joined him on the Cole Porter standard "I've Got You under My Skin," a

Modish, raffish, his snappy trilby in trademark position back in 1956 in Studio A of Capitol Records.

"must" at every Sinatra concert. Kenny G, another contemporary artist, stamps his cool soprano saxophone sound on "All the Way" and "One for My Baby"; Anita Baker joins him for "Witchcraft"; and Carly Simon joins him for "Guess I'll Hang My Tears Out to Dry" segueing into "In the Wee Small Hours of the Morning."

For more years than some of these singers have been alive, these songs have been food and drink to Sinatra. Emotional studio scenes had attended some of the sessions; grown men, musicians with a lifetime of experiences accompanying the greats, stood to applaud when Frank completed some of the songs. And, quietly, the star must have known that if those potent artists could deliver the goods in the way Ramone and Cattaneo expected, he was on to a rare winner ... rather late in his career.

By the time *Duets* was released towards the end of 1993, Frank Sinatra was already enjoying a reappraisal, and a renewal in his popularity. The sound of his original solo version of "New York, New York" boomed in discos and wine bars the world over; young artists from punk rockers to orchestra musicians and new jazz bands were reinterpreting his work and admitting his importance; and it appeared that, after all the good and the bad, the ugly and the indifferent sounds that pop music had bestowed upon us in the 1960s and beyond, age was suddenly no barrier to popularity. The upsurge of interest in the music of Sinatra was not rooted in nostalgia. Young adults aged between twenty and thirty had discovered crooning, the music of the 1950s, allied to the music of the big bands, as if it were something new. After the Beatles and the Rolling Stones, after acid rock and disco, the orchestral rock of the 1970s and the high decibel count of the 1980s, after hip-hop, grunge, techno and rap, radio stations were getting their strongest listening figures by playing the music of Sinatra, Tony Bennett and artists singing ballads.

As well as confirming Sinatra's artistic fertility, *Duets* proved a monumental commercial success. Adorned by a specially commissioned painting of him by renowned artist LeRoy Neiman, Sinatra looked as he sounded: modish, raffish, snappy trilby in position as if he were fifty years younger. And *Duets* sold millions around the world.

For Capitol Records, Phil Ramone, Hank Cattaneo, Don Rubin and others, it was a blissful vindication. They had smelled success from the start, but with Sinatra nothing was predictable. "It's no hype," Ramone told me. "He's proud of the record. He wanted the record out fast; to him, this is a piece of work! Once he'd done his work, Frank expected to see the record in the stores fast. I met him in a restaurant after he'd finished his work and he said to me: 'Well, we made the album *five weeks ago!* Why isn't it out on the streets?' He would not let anything be released that he did not love. He was *moved* by the work of his duetting partners."

Between 1953 and 1962, Sinatra recorded more than seventeen albums for Capitol during a period that was considered by many people to feature his best work. Ironically, for what some laughingly called his "comeback" album, Capitol invested millions to ensure that it would become the biggest-selling Sinatra album ever, outflanking his best-sellers from the 1950s.

As the dust settled on *Duets,* there were, inevitably, dissenters. Hard-core Sinatra followers judged some of the pairings a mismatch: Streisand and Sinatra together on "I've Got a Crush on You" was called disastrous by Britain's journal of the Sinatra Music Society, which asserted that their man was "groaning and gasping away in the background trying to keep up ... Barbra runs away with the whole thing." The saloon songs, however, notably "One for My Baby," were praised, and in a strangely pernickety summary, the journal of the society (honorary president: Frank Sinatra) described the album as "a worthy addition to the Sinatra library." All those years ago, it observed, Capitol Records had "transformed" Sinatra. "It still does."

The voice, of course, lacks its old firepower, but that scarcely matters if the essence of his art is admired. To millions who have grown up hearing him, from the torch songs on albums like *No One Cares* and *Only the Lonely,* through *Songs for Swingin' Lovers* to *In the Wee Small Hours* and *Trilogy,* Frank Sinatra was never merely a singer. What he represented was at least as crucial: he embodied defiance, braggadocio, hell-raising, arrogance, over-confidence, passion, determination, and was never, but never, indifferent or boring or passive.

The natural strength of his vocal cords has never been the center of any debate about him. It was farcical, therefore, that this should be an issue when the man had entered the recording studio at age seventy-seven. In embarking on the *Duets* project Sinatra was following, intuitively, the road map he alone had constructed six decades earlier: as an individualistic interpreter.

As a singer of songs written by others, Sinatra always played the role of himself. He took total possession, wrapped himself around each and every syllable, grafting his complex

The young Sinatra from Hoboken, New Jersey—perhaps he was born with the trilby.

personality onto the consummate musicianship he learned at the feet of the masters of his era. He has described himself as "the luckiest bum in the world," in referring to the top-class musicians, songwriters and conductors who have surrounded him since his first tentative moves in the music business. Often, though, people make their own luck, and the evidence of Sinatra's formative years points to a restlessness, a yearning for excellence, and a determination to crash through that were irrepressible.

Sinatra was shaped in his birthplace. Hoboken, New Jersey, across the Hudson River from lower New York City, was in 1915 a waterfront square-mile town with a 50,000 population, dense with ethnic minorities: Italians, Poles, Jews and blacks. Its industrial base stemmed from the cargo ships that packed the mile-long waterfront. It was something of a small American Liverpool, ironic in view of the monumental contribution to music and popular culture that was to be provided by both cities.

He was born on 15 December 1915 to Natalie and Martin Sinatra, both immigrants. His father was Sicilian, born in Catania, while his mother, whom everyone called Dolly, came from Genoa. Weighing in at a formidable thirteen and a half pounds, baby Frank was scarred at birth by a forceps delivery, and the marks on the left side of his head and neck would always remain visible. "People have suggested to me I ought to hide those scars," he told author Robin Douglas-Home in 1962. "But no. They're there and that's that. Why bother?"

Monroe Street, baby Sinatra's first home, close to the Erie and Lackawanna railroad, was a low-income area but his parents worked hard to provide well for their only child. Martin Sinatra, whose mild manner concealed his determination, worked as a boilermaker and bartender and eventually for the town's fire department, where he rose to the position of captain. Frank's mother, Dolly, a popular local nurse, was to imbue young Frank with characteristics that would mark his life: drive, ambition and a meticulousness in everything he approached. His sense of tidiness, sartorial pride and need to meticulously chart every action of his life was instilled into him from childhood.

He inherited something special from both parents: piercing blue eyes that were to become part of his trademark appeal. It was not a music-conscious house, but when Frank went to David E. Rue Junior High School, which he left in January 1931, he began to take an interest in music. Later that year he left Demarest High School—where he had sung in the glee club—and went to Drake Business School, his eye vaguely on a professional career. When he showed artistic leanings by doing some sketches of bridges, tunnels and highways, his father was encouraged, hoping that Frank was heading for the highly rated Stevens Institute of Technology in Hoboken. But Frank began singing on street corners with his friends, and the die was cast for a life in music. His father was very disappointed but his mother, who enjoyed watching from afar the world of show business, encouraged him. His lack of a more extended education would cause him regrets later in life, but his ears were becoming attuned to the sounds on the radio that would chart his future.

The loner in Sinatra was formed in those years. "I never had any brothers or sisters," he said many years later. "In my neighborhood every family had twelve kids and they fought constantly. But whenever there was a beef or a party, you never saw such closeness." Perhaps because of this solitary start in life, punctuated by many teenage fights, Sinatra especially valued the intensity of his show-business friendships.

The earliest music to enter Frank's psyche came from the radio in his bedroom. Bing Crosby, Rudy Vallee and Russ Columbo were the talented crooners of the day. The gift of a ukulele from an uncle encouraged Frank to play, although his father had thought after he quit school that he might be interested in becoming a professional boxer. But with his wiry frame and his curly, dark hair already highly attractive to the girls, Frank set his sights on a career in show business. Through his mother's connections as a political activist, he managed to get some small singing engagements at Democrat Party rallies. Now singing at parties, he was gaining confidence in himself, and his keen sense of self, plus his blue-eyed swagger, made him a hit with the girls.

His first job, at eighteen, was in the circulation department of the *Jersey Observer.* He earned $11 a week throwing bundles of papers into delivery trucks, but neither this, nor his step up to the job of copy boy, persuaded him that a life in newspapers was for him.

Sinatra's tributes, in later years, to all his professional colleagues obscure the thrust to carve his career that came from him alone.

This was not a promising time to embark on a career in show business. The early years of the Depression, following the Wall Street Crash of 1929, meant that every corner of the entertainment world was concerned with survival rather than expansion. Dance bands, a launching pad to which every singer had to aspire, were collapsing as people tightened their purses. In 1932, the very year Frank Sinatra decided that his future had to be as a singer, sales of single records in the US hit an all-time low figure of six million. Five years earlier, the figure had been 104 million. (After the Depression, the revival sent figures back up to around 140 million in 1942.)

Conversely, the artists who broke through to success did extremely well. Welcomed as a pleasurable antidote to the solemn mood of the country, dance bands and their singers who found a niche were celebrated heroically.

Mass communication across the US, in the form of the networks NBC and CBS, had begun in 1927 and 1928 respectively, and the jukebox arrived, to further boost popular music during the 1930s. Penetrating the leisure time of even the smallest American rural communities, it opened up new potential for disc sales and laid the foundation for the start of the hit parade.

The singer who became the catalyst to young Frank's dreams was Bing Crosby. By 1932, he was the biggest solo male vocalist in the US. With a beautiful, pure baritone voice, Crosby tapped the nation's need for romance on his hit ballads "Just One More Chance" and "I've Found a Million Dollar Baby," marking an outstanding show-business career that would influence many singers across four decades.

In March 1932, sixteen-year-old Frank Sinatra went to see Crosby's show in Jersey City. The show fuelled Sinatra's determination to "make it" as a singer. The ace that Sinatra unwittingly held for eventually outstripping even Crosby's iron grip on the population was bound up in his personality. Crosby and other successful singers of the era, like Russ Columbo ("Prisoner of Love") and Gene Austin ("My Blue Heaven"), sold their songs. Their voices were excellent and true, their personalities pleasant. Sinatra studied them all, analyzing in his mind the qualities that made them great. Crosby, as the biggest star, interested him particularly, but Frank knew there was little point in emulating him. A fresh ingredient would be essential to be a successful crooner. "I decided to experiment a little and come up with something different," he told *Life* magazine in 1965. "What I finally hit on was the more bel canto Italian school of singing. I had to stay in better shape because I had to sing more." One of his methods of staying in shape during his Hoboken years was to swim under water, which improved his breath control.

These were the scuffling years. Watching his ascent, it has been too easy to forget the hard times. Desperate to get a foothold with an established big band, Sinatra knew that being heard was the key. And it was difficult. After a spell touring with the Hoboken Four, a vocal-instrumental quartet, which gave him club work across the country, he decided he *had* to get on the radio, the medium that had delivered Crosby and Rudy Vallee to success.

In a startlingly bold move, when he left the *Jersey Observer* payroll, he approached program directors at radio stations like WOR in Newark, New Jersey, and WNEW in New York, offering to sing without a fee. He was used as a "filler"; eventually, he could be heard on the air crooning the hits of the day eighteen times a week. This gruelling, dollarless, self-imposed training equipped him well for much of what would follow. Eventually he was all over the radio on the East Coast, making a particularly significant impact with listeners on the cigarette-sponsored series *Lucky Strike Hit Parade*. Radio and television were to be crucial to his burgeoning popularity in his formative decades; in the 1950s, Frank would feature on five nationally networked television series.

What drove him? Here was an eighteen-year-old from the rough streets of Hoboken freed of the draft because of a punctured eardrum, striving to reach the top with no contacts in the higher echelons of show business. Then, as now, Sinatra was never one to be beaten down; the verve of his later performances was inside the "skinny Italian kid," as he sang of himself, even at that stage in his personal life.

Winning an amateur talent contest at the State in Jersey City got him a chance to sing at the well-established Academy of Music on 14th Street in Manhattan. He did not win there, but he used the springboard to build friendships with song pluggers and others in New York's Tin Pan Alley. He was on his way, albeit slowly.

Next he secured a vital residency at a tavern called the Rustic Cabin, on Route 9 West, near Englewood Cliffs, New Jersey. For $15 a week, Frank sang solo, sang with a group, often acted as master of ceremonies and sometimes doubled as a waiter. The songs in his repertoire, "Love Me or Leave Me" and "That Old Black Magic," gave him scope to present a more muscular alternative to Bing Crosby. Young, thin, vulnerable, and with a deliberation in his vocal phrasing that owed little

The Hoboken Four with a local theater manager. The gift of a ukulele from an uncle led Sinatra to the group and to gigs around the country.

to the established giants, he was acknowledged by many local musicians as way ahead of his years … and of them.

The vital rung on the ladder to success came after eighteen months of slogging away at the Rustic Cabin. Harry James, the trumpet-playing leader of one of the hottest bands of the period, came off stage one night during his stint at New York's Paramount Theatre and entered his dressing room. On the radio, he heard on WNEW's Dance Parade program the voice of an unknown. James recognized talent; he asked the radio station who the boy Frank Sinatra was, and how he could be contacted. Then he took a cab to the Rustic Cabin to see the show.

To complete this fairy-tale scenario, James offered Sinatra a two-year contract with his excellent, well-respected band at the rate of $75 a week.

At his opening with the Harry James Band at the Hippodrome, Baltimore, in June 1939, Sinatra's name was so unknown that he was not even billed. But he received

Radio was the perfect medium for Sinatra, crucial to the momentum of his burgeoning popularity.

rapturous receptions and, as a pointer, he proved especially attractive to female fans. This was by no means predictable for a pop singer in those pre-rock 'n' roll years; the musicians found it a remarkable phenomenon, attributable to Sinatra's lean good looks and youth rather than to his ability to communicate through songs.

Sinatra was twenty-three now, and had every reason to be self-satisfied. Four months before joining the James band, he had married. After a five-year romance that had begun on a vacation, Frank had wed Nancy Barbato, a year younger than himself, in a traditional Italian Catholic wedding at Our Lady of Sorrows Church in Jersey City on 4 February 1939. Living in a three-roomed apartment in Jersey City, the couple were separated by Frank's interminable travelling as the James band claimed him for coast-to-coast travel. But he phoned Nancy nightly. Working as a $25-a-week secretary, she supported and encouraged him in his quest for success.

It was an era of sweet-sounding big band music, of Glenn Miller and Benny Goodman, of tunes like "In the Mood" and ballads like "Begin the Beguine," which Sinatra perfected to his own narrative style. Inside the James band, where he shared the vocal job with Connie Kay, he built his popularity. And he was hungry to learn. Though James was more popular as a trumpeter than his band was as a unit, the musicianship around Frank spurred him to do something that not every singer did: he *listened.* Surrounded by guys who had been "working the road" for years, Frank was absorbed by their prowess. Here, and in the next job he had, was where Sinatra's genius was to be perfected: he would sculpt his voice as an instrument, gliding around the lyric rather than hitting the notes as they were written.

By the end of 1939, though, the Harry James Band was in economic trouble. And when Nancy, who had travelled with her husband on the road for a while, told him she was pregnant, Frank said the road was no place for her. She returned to Jersey City.

The seven months he spent with Harry James from June 1939 exposed Frank to an extraordinary array of talent, which fuelled his ambition as a father-to-be. Visiting Chicago in September 1939 with the James band, who were playing the Panther Room at the Hotel Sherman, Sinatra heard that Billie Holiday was playing a few dates at the Off Beat Room, the small downstairs section of the Three Deuces Club. On several nights, sitting watching her intently, Sinatra absorbed the vocal artistry of a woman whose imprimatur on jazz interpretation was a precursor to his own on popular singing. Like Sinatra was to do in the future, she poured every nuance of her soul into each word, taking full ownership of her songs. Acknowledging her influence on his work in 1958, Frank stated: "Billie Holiday was, and still remains, the greatest single musical influence on me. Lady Day is unquestionably the most important influence on American popular singing in the last twenty years."

Creatively, after seven months traversing the country, Frank had outgrown the James band, and set his sights elsewhere. On that same visit to Chicago, he went across to the Palmer House to see and hear the band led by Tommy Dorsey. Sinatra was always mightily impressed by virtuoso musicianship that combined a touch of showmanship. In Tommy Dorsey, he found both—and he wanted a job in that "happening band." There was a problem, however: Dorsey had a splendid singer, Jack Leonard, who was pretty popular and had enjoyed a hit with a song called "Marie." For three successive years he had won the male singer section in popularity polls run by major magazines *Down Beat* and *Metronome*. Leonard also enraptured a strong female crowd and was a hot property for Dorsey. But fate was about to smile on Sinatra. It was time for Jack Leonard to spread his wings. He quit Dorsey to go solo. That left the berth for the male vocalist in the best band in the land vacant at exactly the moment Frank was hungry for it. Tommy Dorsey's aggregation, as dance bands were often called in those years, was run on strict, disciplinary lines. Dorsey's mellow trombone work led from the front and he tolerated only the highest levels of professionalism. It was a slicker band than James's, fired by the Dorsey trombone, which actually achieved for

Working with Tommy Dorsey had a profound effect on Sinatra: "I may be the only singer who ever took vocal lessons from a trombone."

the instrument a sexuality akin to that of the guitar in rock twenty years later.

Sinatra badly wanted that job with the band that was the most prestigious in the US. Fortunately, during his James years, he had made some singles, straight ballads that caught the ears of the shrewd Dorsey, who sent word to Sinatra that he would like to meet him. That kind of invitation to any singer in 1939 was equivalent to a mountaineer reaching the summit. There was no hotter ticket than the Dorsey band.

Dorsey's offer of $150 a week for a three-year contract was irresistible. As a career move, it

was perfect. As an invitation to a man with a wife three months pregnant, it was a terrific boost. (Frank and Nancy's daughter, Nancy Sandra, was born on 8 June 1940.) Frank went to see Harry James, with whom his contract had eighteen months to run. James knew the strength of the move and told Frank: "You're free."

As the years passed, Sinatra would sometimes be depicted as a heartless bully, but his departure from James provided an early example of the deep emotion in the man that would find articulacy in his work. The James band had provided him with a magic carpet ride into show business, and he was touched by the grace shown by Harry in freeing him to join Dorsey. Remembering the moment of departure later, Frank recalled the final separation after the last show in Buffalo, New York: "It was after midnight. There was nobody around and I stood alone with my suitcase in the snow and watched the tail-light of the [band] bus disappear. Then the tears started… and I tried to run after the bus."

The effect of Tommy Dorsey on twenty-five year-old Frank Sinatra was profound. What Frank needed to point him skywards was the wisdom, personality, and uncompromising example of an older man at the top of his craft who commanded respect. In Dorsey, the fiercely ambitious Sinatra met his alter ego.

So far, Frank had been a strong singer within a band. The Dorsey experience was to teach him to step outside himself, to implant his mercurial, passionate determination in ballads that Dorsey chose with immense skill. There was other chemistry at work to clinch Sinatra's emergence: shoulder to shoulder with Dorsey and with musicians like the battling drummer Buddy Rich and pitch-perfect singer Jo Stafford in the band bus, Sinatra was in the company of utter perfectionists. Dorsey carried no passengers, and with a temper at least equivalent to Frank's, the scene was set for the most turbulent roller coaster in Sinatra's young life.

Nancy as secretary and supporter worked far beyond the call of duty.

Casual and slovenly were words that have never entered Sinatra's vocabulary. All his life he would be fastidious about his appearance, his timekeeping, and would pay microscopic attention to detail. He sought exactly the same qualities in those round him, and in Dorsey this self-discipline was essential, too. Gruff and uncompromising, he led by example: an all-time master trombonist, he perfected a mellifluous style as seductive as it was incomparable. His phrasing was unlike that of any other musician as he segued from note to note apparently without drawing breath. If Sinatra was the vocalist with a great natural ear, then Dorsey, ten years his senior, was his equal on his instrument.

Frank was mesmerized by his playing, night after night, as he sat on the bandstand. A voracious appetite for learning from others now fired Sinatra, who relished being in the company of the best in the land. Confirming that Dorsey taught him just about everything he knew about phrasing and breath control, Frank joked to US broadcaster Sid Mark on a series called *Sounds of Sinatra*: "I may be the only singer who ever took vocal lessons from a trombone. Tommy could blow that thing for a week on one tank of air and I latched on to his secret."

Remembering how he sat on the bandstand behind Dorsey as the leader stood playing, Sinatra said: "I used to look at his jacket, figuring if he was going to take a breath, his coat was going to move a little. But it never moved. So I used to lean round to see what he was doing at the front." But as a trombonist, his face was covered by his hand. After about a year and a half of watching and wondering, Frank became impatient, although in view of his temperament, one wonders what took him so long.

Dorsey explained to his young singer that when playing an instrument, he covered the mouthpiece with practically his whole hand. "And he was getting a breath from the corner of his mouth, a quick breath," Sinatra recalled. "He said: 'You cannot possibly do that because you're singing with your mouth wide open. You are going to have to devise another way to do that.' So I did. I started to work on it. I was doing the same thing, except I was not squeezing it in the corner. I was taking a breath normally between syllables."

Dorsey, avers Sinatra, taught him self-discipline above all else. He instilled in him total dedication to every musical detail. That would cause him, in the years after Dorsey, "to respect every record I make as if it's the last song I'll ever sing." Later, acknowledging his debt to musicians, he cited other great instrumentalists who had made an impact on him: violinist Jascha Heifetz, jazz saxophonist Lester Young, "and a lot of soloists who blew horns."

Violinists and cellists intrigued him as a vocalist "because they have that sustained quality of notation…. Heifetz could play a phrase where there was a perceptible feeling that the bow across the strings never broke; it went from one note to another and … there was never a feeling of it stopping."

Sinatra worked incredibly hard with Dorsey. His smooth, tentative voice, the young version of what would later captivate millions, found its first recorded outlet supported by the cool arrangements of the Dorsey band.

Classic ballads like "Stardust," "I'll be Seeing You," "Polka Dots and Moonbeams," "Imagination" and "East of the Sun" gave Frank scope to hone the style he wanted. In all, he recorded some eighty discs with Dorsey. There was even a song that hit the top of the best-seller charts. "I'll Never Smile Again" stayed at the top for seven weeks, from July 1940.

By the end of that year, Frank knew he was now on the way to being a true star. His skinny physique scored a direct hit on girls, who were swooning as he walked up to the microphone. This displeased two men in particular: Tommy Dorsey probably saw the storm clouds looming, and was possessive enough of his band as a unit to resent the sweep to popularity of the kid singer, and it also irritated the brilliant, powerhouse drummer Buddy Rich. Two years younger than Frank, Rich was the most dynamic drummer in the genre, and he knew it. As he watched Sinatra's cocksure ascent, he made it clear that a takeover of the Dorsey band by Sinatra was not going to happen. There were tensions, and Rich played havoc with the tempo on some songs to spite Sinatra. Later, however, Rich and Sinatra became firm friends.

Now came the plaudits that would make Sinatra's position in the Dorsey line-up unassailable. An annual survey in *Billboard* magazine in May 1941 named Frank as top band vocalist, and a few months later *Down Beat* magazine put him at the top of its readers' poll, knocking aside Bing Crosby, who had won it for three successive years.

As a baritone commanding his field, Sinatra was now respected professionally. As a heartthrob he was eclipsing every other singer in the nation.

His vulnerability, his nervous intensity, his frailty, and now his extraordinary expression in songs of yearning touched all but the stonyhearted. The physical effect on a generation, as Sinatra walked to the microphone night after night with Dorsey to sing

"There Are Such Things," was the first manifestation of the pop idol who merged vocal ability with sex appeal. Before Sinatra band singers were just that—purveyors of songs.

Time magazine featured him on the cover and reported: "Sinatra would appear on stage, looking like a terrified boy of fifteen in the presence of his first major opportunity. His face was like a wet rag. . . . He would hang for a moment on the microphone, holding it itchily, as if it were a snake. His chest caved in, as if from the weight of the enormous zoot suit shoulders it bore and a huge floppy bow tie hung down like the ears of a spaniel. For a moment he would look among his audience, pleadingly, as if searching for his mother, and then he would begin, timidly and with trembling lips, to sing."

There was nothing bashful about the way he sang, often targeting one girl in the audience. Those piercing blue eyes were mesmeric and so was his voice. That way of singling out someone, anyone, and addressing the lovelorn ballads to her was to stand Sinatra apart from many of the other fine singers who handled the songs with immense care, but without passion. Sinatra never merely sang the notes. Even with Dorsey, he was a putative actor with ideas, attack, an indefinable touch.

And so it was that under Dorsey's barnstorming tutelage, Frank's fiery ambition was shaken, stirred, molded. "Tommy taught me everything I knew about singing," Sinatra has said. "He was my real education." The first pop singer to understand the crucial importance of breath control, and to use it for emphasis, Sinatra was now in a league of one.

Inevitably, he had to go solo. Tommy Dorsey, who had noted the singer's rise to the point where the show was virtually becoming "Frank Sinatra and the Tommy Dorsey Band," bowed to Frank's decision, allowing the singer to buy himself out of his contract.

All his life, Frank Sinatra has demonstrated a need to be in charge, to control his own destiny. Quitting Dorsey was dangerous but he carried, now, a considerable army of fans. It was make or break for a twenty-seven-year-old husband and father.

Frank the family man. Here in 1944 with wife Nancy and daughter Nancy, who would become part of the best-selling double act some 20 years on.

Sinatra

The Voice

Defiance and individuality were central to the emergence of Francis Albert Sinatra in his path from New Jersey to California and the world stage. From his earliest years as a band singer, he vowed to be different,

1915-55

stylish, intensely personal in his moving interpretation of songs beautifully crafted by the best writers of the era.

Heading for stardom in the 1940s, he began a parallel career as an actor that would play a major part in his renaissance after a tricky patch. Sinatra always stamped his work and his life with uncompromising passion, which, laced with his artistry and musicianship, would shape the legend.

Frank inherited something special from both parents—
his piercing blue eyes. Martin, his father, became captain
of the Hoboken Fire Department (he is photographed
above in uniform) and Dolly, a popular local nurse,
imbued her son with drive, ambition, and sartorial
pride—he was known as Slacksy as a teenager because
his mother bought him so many pairs of slacks.

**In *Anchors Aweigh*
Sinatra co-starred
with Gene Kelly and
Kathryn Grayson.**

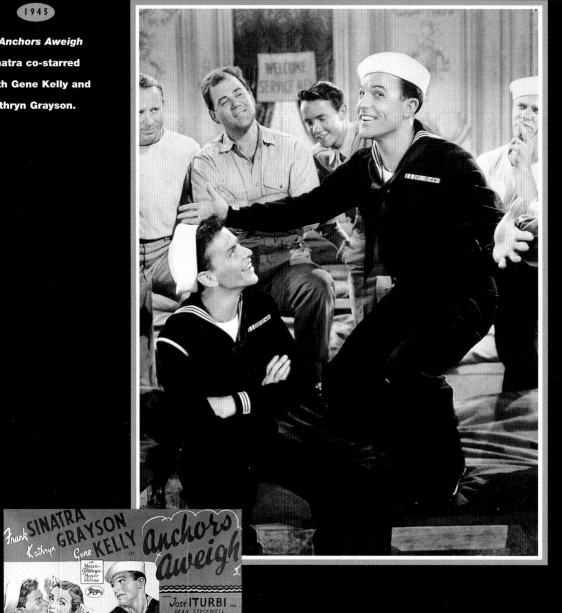

**His vulnerability
and extraordinary
power of expression
touched all but the**

1948

In *Take Me Out to the Ball Game*, Sinatra and Gene Kelly battled for the favors of the baseball club's new owner, played by Esther Williams.

1950

First night at the London Palladium, where Sinatra made his British stage debut.

1955

Young at Heart,
with its sentimental
storyline, was
redeemed by the
singing of Sinatra
and Doris Day.

1949

Meeting Ava Gardner at a film première just before Christmas 1949 proved a timely part in his life and career. The alchemy between them proved inspirational. His obsession with Ava ultimately inspired Sinatra to triumph over adversity.

1951

Meet Danny Wilson combined mobster melodrama with a number of coolly delivered standards in Sinatra's easy style.

The classic Capitol albums, *Songs for Young Lovers*, *In the Wee Small Hours*, and *Swing Easy*, in 1954, allowed Sinatra and his new producer Nelson Riddle to concentrate on mood set pieces. The two were fully able to exploit the new potential of the recently introduced long-playing album.

1955

In *Guys and Dolls*, Brando played
Sky Masterson and Sinatra, Nathan
Detroit, roles that Sinatra would
have preferred reversed. He was
right on this occasion—his
portrayal proved more Sicilian than
Jewish. The Brando "method"
approach was anathema to Frank
and they did not get on. Here they
are with co-stars Jean Simmons
(left) and, from the original stage-
production, Vivien Blaine.

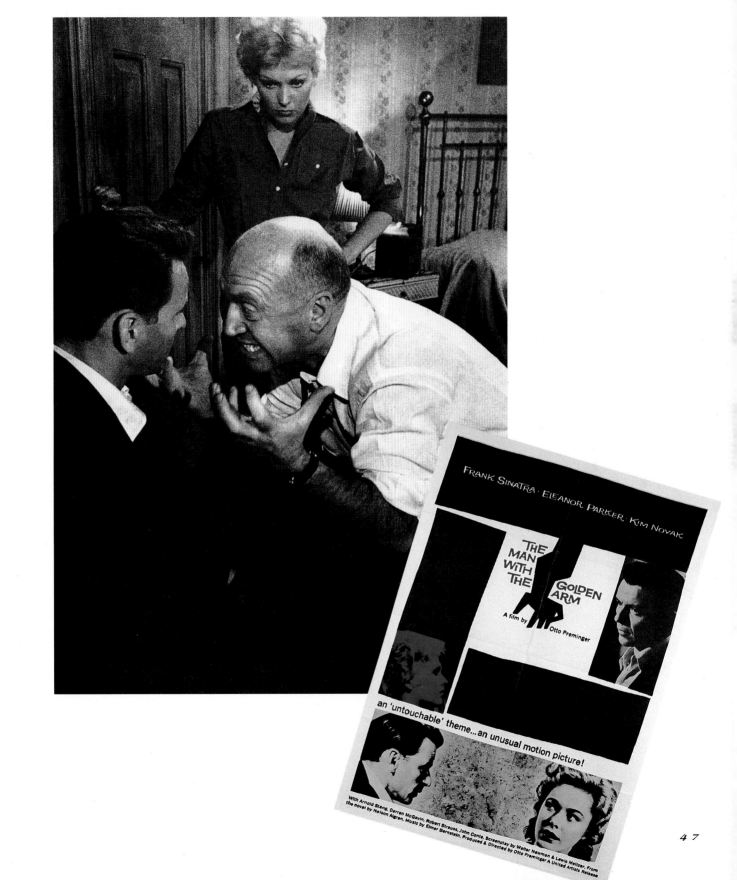

1955

An Oscar nomination
came with his
portrayal of a
drug-addicted poker
dealer in *The Man
with the Golden Arm*.
The award that year
went to Ernest
Borgnine for *Marty*,
but depite Otto
Preminger's heavy-
handed direction,
Sinatra's performance
was full of integrity
and established his
potential as a serious
screen actor.

FRANK SINATRA · ELEANOR PARKER · KIM NOVAK

THE MAN WiTH THE GOLDEN ARM

A film by Otto Preminger

an 'untouchable' theme... an unusual motion picture!

With Arnold Stang, Darren McGavin, Robert Strauss, John Conte. Screenplay by Walter Newman & Lewis Meltzer. From the novel by Nelson Algren, Music by Elmer Bernstein, Produced & Directed by Otto Preminger A United Artists Release

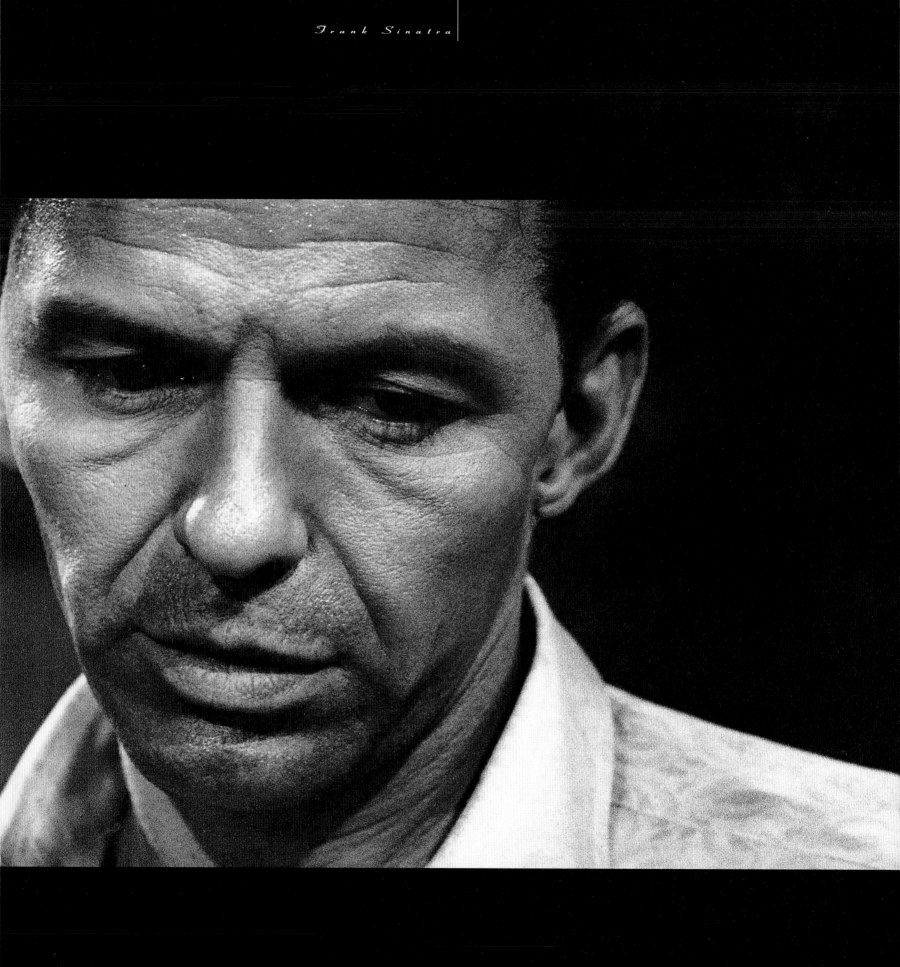

Nice 'n' Easy

His task was both simple and daunting: effectively to rewrite the textbook of popular singing and, in doing so, to eclipse the great Bing Crosby. For a romantic like Frank Sinatra, this must have seemed a weird irony. Ten years earlier, as a Hoboken teenager, Frank had had a picture of Bing on the wall in the bedroom of his home. Frank even smoked a pipe, Crosby style. Bing's wonderfully pure baritone voice had dominated popular song since 1930 when he had left his training ground, the Rhythm Boys, a unit within the popular Paul Whiteman Band.

Both his acting and singing had matured. Left: Mean and moody in *The Man with the Golden Arm* and, right, taking over from Crosby, the two contenders seen here on the road with Bob Hope.

A string of wistful ballads, sung in an easily identifiable light and airy style, had ingrained Crosby's voice into the national consciousness: "Where the Blue of the Night Meets the Gold of the Day," "Wrap Your Troubles in Dreams," "White Christmas," "Love in Bloom," "Temptation," "Please," "It's Easy to Remember"… the list was formidable. A national institution, Bing was the apogee of popular music and a safe, reassuring sound for an America that wanted to expunge the reality of Pearl Harbor and war from its collective consciousness. As Sinatra planned his solo outing, two factors about Bing occurred to Frank: enduring though he would always be, he had not been properly challenged. And, though he was a master vocalist, he did not have much personal magnetism. Crosby relied entirely on the weight of his songs and his avuncularity to clinch his success. He was cosy, nonthreatening; Frank would turn out to be precisely the opposite.

Crosby had been as perfect for his time as Sinatra was to prove as the 1940s unfolded. The sceptics who wondered if he could survive outside the Dorsey umbrella did not have to wait long. On 30 December 1942, billed as an "Extra Added Attraction," Sinatra opened alongside the Benny Goodman Sextet and singer Peggy Lee at the Paramount Theatre on Times Square, New York. It was a prestige solo début at the turn of the year, and Frank was in strong musical company. Goodman's introduction of Sinatra was an understated: "And now, Frank Sinatra." The roar from the crowd was "tremendous," Sinatra recalled later. He was "scared stiff… I couldn't move a muscle… Benny froze, too. He turned round, looked at the audience and asked: 'What the hell is that?'" Sinatra laughed and pressed into an upbeat song, "For Me and My Gal."

Sinatra fever was born that night. The era of the bobbysoxer, a quaint word that characterized the shrieking young women by the ankle sox they all wore, was heralded by Frank as he tore conscientiously through his set, scarcely audible over the screams. Peggy Lee recalled in her autobiography: "We used to lean out the windows of the dressing rooms to see the crowds of swooners, like swarms of bees down there in

Sinatra fever: the young heartthrob is mobbed by fans after a performance.

the street, just waiting for the sight of Sinatra. It must have been unimaginably exciting for him … his days filled with interviews and autographs and all the things that go with the fireworks of sudden fame."

As wild scenes continued nightly, with about 25,000 people clamoring in Times Square, and Sinatra's personal security stepped up to usher him through stage door crowds desperate for a look, a touch, or a tug at his sleeve, America awoke to its new phenomenon. Sociologists tried to explain the bizarre mentality of young girls and older women for whom Frank was a demi-god.

"It was electric when Frank came out on stage," Peggy Lee wrote. She described, too, Frank's compassion when she developed influenza during the Paramount season. Sinatra discovered she was in her dressing room feeling ill, "and from that time until I was well, he was my special nurse. He brought me blankets to stop the shivering. Then, when it was possible, a little tea, later a piece of toast. Meantime, he was out there singing six or eight shows a day in that huge theatre with the cheering crowds—'All or Nothing at All,' 'I'll Never Smile Again.'"

Sinatra had shown her many kindnesses, but Peggy remembered especially what he had done for her in the middle of that first triumphant season. "He could have been too busy, but he wasn't."

In similar scenes during his eight weeks at the Paramount at the start of 1943, Sinatra laid claim to Crosby's crown as the number one singer in America. Bing's unswerving followers maintained that with the warmth of his vocals he would always be more faithful to the songs than the "new boy." But there was no contest: with Sinatra's physical appeal matched to his strong sharp individuality, he offered the public something unique. His originality owed nothing to popular music history; even in 1943, he was a one-off. "Who's best? Sinatra or Crosby?" was a hollow debate with no real validity; the two giants had an entirely different appeal. As the years passed they became friends and Crosby's career was scarcely diminished by Frank's arrival. Sinatra had quite brilliantly masterminded his overtaking of the singer known as "The Old Groaner."

As the hysteria for Frank became hotly debated by all the media, one theory was that his timing to go solo was perfect: with husbands thousands of miles away at war, twenty-seven-year-old Frank provided a natural figure for women to cling to. He sang straight to their emotionally starved hearts.

True in part, this overlooked the potent cocktail he had self-consciously developed through years of study, self-awareness, and experience in the hard training camps of the James and Dorsey bands. He had an immediately identifiable voice that sang smooth ballads with feeling and upbeat songs with flair; and he had married it to his swaggering personality. With the phrasing that he had learned from Billie Holiday, it combined into an unrepeatable package. Through the years, many of Frank's lieutenants have been credited with helping to steer him upwards: from musicians to press agents, from song pluggers to writers. In truth, he was the only significant architect of his success.

Returning to the Paramount in October 1944, Sinatra showed that his first triumph there had been no hype. The 3,600-seat venue was too small to satisfy the estimated 30,000 fans who formed gigantic queues along 44th Street and Eighth Avenue. Statistically, the concert disappointed ten times more ticketless fans than it satisfied, but those who went confirmed Frank's new status as the biggest idol in the US. The fans were described as "scream-agers."

Although idolatry was not new (Al Jolson and Rudolph Valentino had both been lesser focal points before Sinatra), the degree by which Sinatra broke the records was astounding. If Crosby, his immediate predecessor, had become popular by sounding comfortable, Frank was iconoclastic. Not until the onslaught of rock 'n' roll in the 1950s was there anything comparable. Then, coincidentally, the concerts at the same Paramount, hosted by legendary disc jockey Alan Freed of radio station WINS, came close to the Sinatra fever.

Dissecting the phenomenon gave writers ample scope for subjectivity. It was, said some, a *cri de coeur* from girls who were starved of affection. It was a million females fantasizing about their sexual desires. While one critic wrote about the "quiver at the corner of the mouth" that was central to Sinatra's appeal, a less visual element seemed to be ignored. Sinatra was a slender, jaunty figure who, aside from his blue-chip talent, represented the ordinary guy taking on the world. His public image was one of a battler who had paid his dues and had now come to collect. America lauds success, and Sinatra had every piece of equipment in the armory.

New York's famous Paramount Theatre, in 1944, stormed by 30,000 fans during a Sinatra engagement.

Yet while his stardom was secured by his live shows, the route to longevity lay in records. With the Harry James Band, Frank made his début with "From the Bottom of My Heart" on Brunswick, a subsidiary of the Columbia label, plus "It's Funny to Everyone but Me," "My Buddy," and "All or Nothing at All." In the Dorsey band, in what was a credit line of the time, his name appeared under the Dorsey name as "Vocal Chorus: Frank Sinatra." But with a profitable RCA Victor contract, Dorsey was predictably prolific and Frank's recording experience received its true foundation. He made about 100 commercial records with the Dorsey band and appeared also on V-Discs, which were special discs not available commercially, but distributed to US Forces.

Because of Frank's popularity, song pluggers had approached him as well as the band leader with material, to the chagrin of Tommy. Frank's unerring ear for a song that had the right "feel" for him, as well as for the musicianly approach of Tommy's men, proved a winning formula. Heard now, the voice of Sinatra on "Fools Rush In," "I'll be Seeing You," "Stardust" (which he once described as the most difficult song to sing, ever), "Oh Look at Me Now" and "Everything Happens to Me" is a clear signal of his ability to maintain, in the grooves of a record, the ingredients he gave to every song on the concert platform.

As he had begun his solo career, Sinatra and his aides had presented him as "The Voice That Thrills Millions." That phrase applied comfortably to him on the road, where "thrills" was an understatement. Now, for the recording aspect of his career, he was simply "The Voice."

Since the first break at the Rustic Cabin, his master plan had worked perfectly. Frank was earning an estimated million dollars a year, and it was time to upgrade the marital home where Nancy had raised their daughter. For she was now pregnant again.

The East Coast was still Frank's essential base. Geographically, in those years, the recording industry was located there; movie stars, rather than singers and musicians, belonged in Hollywood. And both Frank and Nancy felt comfortable in the New Jersey area. Their new home was at 220 Lawrence Avenue, Hasbrouck Heights. This was solid commuter territory, and for a while, as he stepped up his recording output, Frank appeared to revel in domesticity, setting up home, enjoying Nancy's classic Italian cooking, and being a proud father. Their second child, Frank Junior, was born at Margaret Hague Maternity Hospital, Jersey City, on 10 January 1944. Frank was yet to have any brushes with the media, and even welcomed photographers to his home, pronouncing the publicity as beneficial to his career.

They photographed the proud father, who also did a spot of lawn mowing. The birth of his son came at another turning point in Frank's rocketing story. At the end of December 1943, the respected music magazine *Down Beat* announced that he was the most popular singer in its annual poll; he easily beat Bing Crosby and Perry Como, as well as Dick Haymes, who had succeeded him in the Dorsey Band.

At the start of the new year, Sinatra continued his activities in the world of movies, which had begun during his period with the Dorsey band. In 1940, Dorsey had filmed *Las Vegas Nights*, which featured Frank; it was his first movie part, and two years later, *Ship Ahoy* gave him another lightweight part, dressed as a sailor.

His film career gathered pace in the early 1940s in tandem with nightclub dates, concert work, and crucially important coast-to-coast radio series, notably the *Lucky Strike Hit Parade.* His third movie, *Reveille with Beverly,* was quickly followed by his first real starring role, in RKO Radio's *Higher and Higher.*

His movie appearances continued apace, with *Step Lively* followed in 1945 by the first appearance of any significance in *Anchors Aweigh,* which co-starred Gene Kelly and Kathryn Grayson. On 7 March 1946, Sinatra received a special Academy Award for his appearance in a short movie, *The House I Live In.* With its theme of patriotism and opposition to racial bigotry, it was the first pronouncement by the star that he wanted to display a social conscience.

These movies presaged a broadening of his horizons away from music, and, with hindsight, seem to have been unwise diversions. Thus far, Frank was not a significant actor, and his avowed aim of being the biggest singer on earth needed consolidation. Adults who had grown up with Bing Crosby refused to be drawn to the more glamorous Sinatra, but in spite of efforts to spark controversy, Sinatra always spoke warmly of Bing: "Bing was my first singing idol. And he still is. He'll always be tops … there's no comparison between us. We're entirely different in style." Frank was wise to acknowledge Bing's staying power. For while Sinatra shone, Crosby was an immovable force, churning out hits like "Pennies from Heaven," "Love in Bloom" and "Please…" and notching up a raft of movie hits including the 1944 Academy Award winner, *Going My Way,* and his own Oscar for best actor.

By a neat coincidence, when Frank made the inevitable move at that time from New Jersey to California he chose for himself, Nancy and their children a house in the swish Toluca Lake district of the San Fernando Valley, in which Crosby was ensconced. Sinatra's

beautiful rendition of the song "Nancy (With the Laughing Face)," a celebration of his daughter, evoked the happiness of a man who had the world on a string. Becoming something of a signature song at the time, it also strengthened his appeal to adults. There was a distinct need for this: as a serious singer, Frank could not for long be seen to appeal just to young women. Inevitably, as they grew older, they would move away. A degree of "crossover" was necessary in marketing him. Those early movies were time-wasting, and out of focus.

Stars of Sinatra's magnitude are born rather than manufactured. Often, the environment in which they grew up has shaped both their outlook, and by virtue of it, their art. Elvis Presley was always, palpably, a boy from Tupelo, Mississippi; the Beatles remain quintessential Liverpudlians. Frank Sinatra was a sharp-tongued battler from the streets of Hoboken.

His notorious temper was fired by his hatred of racial slurs: as he recalled, if you were called a "Guinea," or a "Dago," both slights against his Italian lineage, there was only one way to respond: with your fists. As his profile glittered in Hollywood, his spats with journalists—and with rowdy members of the audiences at his concerts or in restaurants—presented a hubristic image. Incident by incident, it matters not, contextually, whether

Sinatra was right; but his stance is relevant to the story as it affects his work. Since the Voice is unmistakably the Man, its ingredients must always have had a caustic edge as well as a large dose of romance. In public, Sinatra's image has always been that of the swashbuckling hero, the enthusiastic lover who knew all about those sad love songs because he'd been down that road so many times himself.

Sinatra quite early got under the skin of journalists, and vice versa. He would probably have preferred that not to happen, but confrontations with the media through the years have worked to his advantage. He has emerged as a sharp-shooter who will take nothing from anyone, particularly from the press. He has maintained that while his public career as an artist is open for comment, his private life is inviolate and he is entitled to lock the door. And where that division is demarcated, he has insisted, impractically, is his domain. Such intractability could never work. Aside from the media's nosy ground rules, would Frank have preferred his world travels for charity to have gone unreported?

He once wore a T-shirt with the slogan: GOSSIP WRITERS STINK. One of Sinatra's most comprehensive and objective biographers, Arnold Shaw, reports how, in one of Frank's lighter asides about a writer who had infuriated him, the singer told a nightclub audience during his show that the writer … "isn't here. She's out shopping for a new chin." Stories about his punch-ups with the press punctuate many biographies. As well as showing Sinatra's ire, they also reveal a delicious sense of humor. Shaw tells how, in 1961, Frank "traded blows" with a TV impresario who had invited him to participate in a discussion about "Sinatra and the Clan."

When Frank cabled back that his fee was $250,000 an hour, the TV man wired back: "Presume stipulated fee is for your traditional program of intramural ring-a-ding-ding-ing with additional fillip of musical lyrics mounted on teleprompter. Please advice price for spontaneous discussion."

The response was pure Sinatra: "The $250,000 fee is for my usual talent of song and dance. However, now that I understand the picture a little more clearly, I must change it to $750,000 for all parasitical programs."

There was a theory that George Evans, Sinatra's imaginative press agent from 1943 until he died in 1950, orchestrated the manic behavior of fans by paying them to scream and faint. He certainly played a big part in orchestrating the press reportage of Sinatra's ascent.

Seen here escaping the set of the disastrous movie *The Kissing Bandit.* Sinatra's barren years of 1948–9 were perhaps summed up by the song title performed in the film, "What's Wrong With Me?"

Then, as now, the media tended to turn on Sinatra and, rather than celebrate his triumphs, criticize the star once he had reached a pinnacle. At that point, the focus became his off-stage dynamics rather than his ability to sing a song. And yet media attention for his affairs and his antics with the Clan, and for many of his other activities, all helped to build the Sinatra persona. A cooing lover who sang love songs beautifully would never be enough. The man lived in the fast lane, and reporters chased him down it. The oxygen of publicity may have riled him, but it served to help establish his short fuse. That, too, was and is evident in his singing.

In 1947, the year Frank Sinatra Day was proclaimed in Hoboken, Frank recorded nearly seventy songs. These were innocuous, melodic efforts of the style of his earliest signature song, "Put Your Dreams Away," and "I Only Have Eyes for You." Even with these, Frank employed a vocal coating that was the opposite of glossy but was never abrasive. Importantly, he defined his own personality in song: the instant you heard one note, it was attitudinal, questioning, communicative. That elusive, central strength in his appeal had yet to mature. But as his caustic profile sharpened around California, as he fired off feisty telegrams to columnists chiding them for "printing lies," the double-edged reputation of the great artist of the future was developing. Many of his predecessors and contemporaries in show business would passively accept bad press. Sinatra branded most journalists as misrepresenting liars.

As Frank and Nancy's third child, Christina (later known as Tina), was born on 20 June 1948 in Cedars of Lebanon Hospital, Hollywood, his career began to dip. At war's end, the mood was one of rehabilitation and celebration. And for millions who had swooned at his feet, there was no longer loneliness as their men returned home.

Journeying to his summit, Frank had touched people with melodrama and romanticism. "There was great loneliness," he said, explaining his appeal to some degree. "I was the boy in every corner drugstore." Maternalism played its part too.

Now, many of those young girls had grown up, were raising families or cementing real relationships with husbands rather than fantasizing through Frank. And there was the cyclical nature of a show business in which the long-playing record had yet to make its true impact. New artists were emerging, and if they weren't as profound as Sinatra, they came with catchy hits. It was a gimmicky period in popular music, a time when corporate thinking rather than individualism or creativity ruled. Hits were planned and achieved according to formula. Frankie Laine's powerhouse voice belted out "Jezebel," "New Orleans," and "The Kid's Last Fight." Rosemary Clooney, a quality singer, scored with the novelty, "Come-on-a-my-house." Hank Williams, a future legend of country and western music, was demonstrating that what some called hillbilly music was not hokey. On the horizon was Johnnie Ray, a soulful singer who once said he cried real tears on stage, so moved was he by the lyrics of his multi-million-selling tear-jerking ballads "The Little White Cloud That Cried" and "Cry."

Strong ballad singers abounded too: rich baritone voices like Al Martino and Tony Martin. And out there still, as the graph of Frank Sinatra's record sales pointed the wrong way, remained Bing Crosby, who had stayed a crooner and was never a heartthrob. Pipe-smoking, golfing, happy-go-lucky Bing endured where the tigerish Frank ran into heavy turbulence. It must have rankled Sinatra, but he never lost his sardonic sense of humor.

Returning to live appearances, Frank found 1948 and 1949 barren years, but enlivened by the purchase of a house in the exclusive Holmby Hills area of Los Angeles, where his neighbor and friend was his movie hero Humphrey Bogart. Musically, it seemed a negative period for him. And his recorded material, including "Some Enchanted Evening" and "That Lucky Old Sun," didn't carry the luster even of what he had sung with Tommy Dorsey. Commentators derided him as a "spent force," and the downward spiral continued when he quit the radio series *Your Hit Parade.*

At end of a decade in which he had been the shooting star, Sinatra appeared to be the meteorite falling to earth. In *Down Beat* magazine's poll, Frank's regular berth, the number one male singer spot, was taken by the theatrical Billy Eckstine, with Frankie Laine second. Joint third place were Bing Crosby and Mel Tormé. Sinatra was a humbling fifth.

The battler was always working, however. There were upsides. His movie career chugged along with a successful appearance in a frothy musical called *On the Town.* This was a surprisingly commercial movie. Although the world still considered him a singer who occasionally acted, even Frank could not have known that the big screen would soon be his salvation.

Simultaneously, his domestic life was in turmoil. Just before Christmas 1949, Frank was in New York at a film première for the show *Gentlemen Prefer Blondes* when he met the woman who was to alter his life. Within weeks, his liaison with Ava Gardner was a gossip columnist's dream. Here was the former heartthrob of millions, suffering what one writer called a "career curve," married, with three children, dining out with the almond-eyed actress. And they were not making much of a secret of it.

His magnificent
obsession with Ava
Gardner was first
publicly appreciated
when Sinatra
attended the
première of MGM's
Showboat with
her in 1951.

Frank appeared in his first British concerts, at the London Palladium, in July 1950. The reception he received was in refreshing contrast to the negativity with which his position was judged in his native land. Ava was in the front row and the alchemy between them might have been inspirational for him; the critics praised his stage magnetism.

Princess Margaret became a public fan. While the *Daily Express* attempted to summarize his appeal as "a thin-faced, tired-looking totem of the tearful," *The Times* got closer to explaining the fragility that lay at the heart of Sinatra's communicative skills: "To a people whose idea of manhood is husky, full-blooded and self-reliant, he has dared to suggest that under the crashing self-assertion, man is still a child, frightened and whimpering in the dark."

Being a good singer was one thing; moving on to greatness was another. Though Sinatra had been regarded as a fine singer for ten years, the 1950s were to ensure that he moved ahead to the status of a giant. His life experience at the start of a new decade when he was thirty-five years old was to fire his muse, enabling him to make that fine crossover from entertainment into art.

This important leap, the fulcrum of Sinatra's work for the next forty-five years, was fuelled by his relationship with Ava Gardner. It is not the function of this portrait of Sinatra to dip into the man's life pruriently; the concern here is his work and the personality that has shaped it. His magnificent obsession with Ava Gardner, however, so elevated Sinatra at a time when he was "down" that it bears some recollection and analysis. A common theory is that his diversion into such a passionate affair adversely affected his career. Hindsight is a wondrous science; I believe the Ava affair was ultimately part of the making of Frank Sinatra.

When they first met, Ava had reportedly "felt an overpowering attraction" for the skinny kid, and 1950 marked their union proper when they took off for Houston, where Frank was appearing in cabaret. In the spring of that year, Sinatra was booked for an important season at New York's famous Copacabana club. "Hurricane Ava," as she was called by some of the media, attended, and they were both booked into the city's Hampshire House. Frank, under medical supervision because of a throat infection, had a bad opening. "This is my first night; give me a break," he pleaded with the audience. But they didn't, and when he made the fatal error of singing the song "Nancy"(about his daughter), some in the crowd laughed at the presence of Ava, who sat close to the front, from where she was giving him encouragement.

Returning after the show to the Hampshire House, Sinatra found that Ava was not there but had gone to a club where her ex-husband, the clarinettist-bandleader Artie Shaw, was playing. Frank was said to have been "screaming with jealousy" when he discovered she had gone. After that, their relationship could only continue tumultuously. The crux of the difficulty in their relationship was Ava's popularity as a film star. Just as Frank's career was at its lowest ebb, hers was flourishing. For a proud man like Sinatra to watch his woman ascend while he was struggling to reassert himself must have been a blow to his ego. And here is the point: it fired him with the determination we saw and heard soon afterwards. The cockiness we were yet to hear on "Come Fly With Me" and "Witchcraft" and "The Tender Trap," the ponderous vocalist we were to love on "Three Coins in the Fountain" and "Here's That Rainy Day" and "Embraceable You," was a man singing with the sound of triumphant determination over adversity. And the Ava affair helped him.

When she flew to Spain to film *Pandora and the Flying Dutchman*, Frank defied the orders of his doctor to stay home and rest his throat, and went with her. This was gallant if not wise; he had lost his voice during a New York performance and many thought the illness was traceable to his psychological stress. Nor was there much solace in Spain. A

Taking tea on the set of *Pandora and the Flying Dutchman* with confidante Mrs Grant of Romulus Pictures. Sinatra was here "for a rest."

Hounded by the Press, they begin to show the tension. While Ava's star was rising, Frank's was bumping along. He partly wrote the great song "I'm A Fool To Want You," which sounded autobiographical to a lot of people.

rumored liaison between Ava and a bullfighter, Mario Cabre, could not be quashed, and the Spanish press proved no better than that in the US at playing a full paparazzi tune.

On holiday in Mexico later, they were hounded by a hundred journalists who wanted to know about Sinatra's marriage to Nancy. While that headed for divorce, Frank invariably looked pale and harassed both in and out of Ava's company. When they finally married on 7 November 1951, in Philadelphia, the wedding was not the secret Frank had wanted. "How did those creeps know where we were?" he demanded.

That year of 1951 offered no warmth to his declining record statistics. At Columbia Records, he came under the aegis of Mitch Miller, a musical director and artists' repertoire man with a musical ear that was commercial but controversial. Among the artists he steered to the top of the best-sellers were Rosemary Clooney, Guy Mitchell and Tony Bennett. But Frank always felt ill at ease with the route Miller charted for him. Too often the songs, such as "Mama Will Bark," were corny. One track, however, garnered Frank critical acclaim for his majestic reading. On the song "I'm a Fool to Want You," which Frank partly wrote, his passion hit a peak that made the lyrics sound almost autobiographically about Ava. Frank's vocal resonated so much that it scarcely sounded like the old Frank. It stands as a unique performance, albeit little known by the public.

And yet, while his career was hardly happening, he needed the press. He offered to be helpful when they wanted him, and sent a conciliatory note to photographers saying: "I'll always be made up and ready in case you want to shoot me," a message that can now be seen as desperate, in the light of his career inactivity. While Ava's star was shining, his own continued to bump around. A season at New York's Paramount, the scene of such triumph for him ten years earlier, brought no ripples. He was not selling many records. His agency reportedly told him they no longer wanted to represent him. Sinatra was down … and though he had secured the prize of Ava, there was the indignity of facing up to her popularity.

Probably for the first and only time in his life and career, Sinatra had lost some of his confidence. Ava, the only constant factor in an embattled and complicated young life, in turn saw him conscientiously keeping an open and responsible relationship with Nancy and his children, for, as Nancy Junior would declare later, he never left the family.

While Frank's record career was in the doldrums, his personal appearances ticked over. In the US, clubs like the Coconut Grove in Hollywood and the Desert Inn in Las Vegas greeted him warmly. But after one such performance, and after an argument at their

Palm Springs home, Ava temporarily moved out and Frank went to live with the songwriter Jimmy Van Heusen.

In November 1952, reunited, Ava Gardner was off to Africa to star with Clark Gable in *Mogambo*. Frank's need to accompany his wife can now be seen as sad and humiliating. While she was regarded as a major actress, filming one of the year's biggest-budget movies, Frank could not even get a role he craved. Before leaving Hollywood, he had been plead-

ing to play the role of Maggio in *From Here to Eternity*. It was only while he was in Kenya in January 1953 that he got a cable offering him the part.

Sinatra had been reading the novel by James Jones about Army life in Hawaii just prior to the bombing of Pearl Harbor, and, as he recalled later: "For the first time in my life I was reading something I really had to do. . . . I knew that if a picture [of the book] was ever made, I was the only actor to play Private Maggio. . . . I knew Maggio. I went to high school with him in Hoboken, I was beaten up with him."

Sinatra hurried back to Hollywood from Nairobi. Now he exhibited the resolve, the hubris, that would set him apart from the pack. He determined to show the world that, far from being beaten, the guy who was down on his luck would be back—and the most spectacular comeback in the history of show business was about to begin.

Marriage to Ava was stormy before, during and after the triumph of his role in *From Here to Eternity*. There were short separations and reunions, with the whole of the Sinatra circle of friends knowing most of the details of the battles. After attending the première of *Mogambo* at Radio City Music Hall in New York, Frank went to Las Vegas to work while Ava went to their home in Palm Springs.

His career now in upswing, their partnership headed inexorably for a split, with the message of that song "I'm a Fool to Want You," which he co-wrote, seeming more relevant. His tortuous relationship with Ava proceeded, but the root of the problem for Frank

After the première of *Mogambo* at Radio City Music Hall, the paths of Frank and Ava divided. Sinatra went to Vegas and work, and his new wife returned home to Palm Springs. Their divorce was announced October 1953.

and Ava was that they were both mercurial artists. What he probably wanted from his wife was compliance, passivity, and unflinching support, particularly during the period when he was on the ropes; Ava felt she was the bigger star at that time. While he was fighting to reposition himself, she had an abundance of work. Egotists by the definition of their careers, they were on a collision course, and by 27 October 1953 it was announced that they were going to divorce.

Shortly afterwards, Sinatra was in a New York hospital suffering from "complete physical exhaustion, severe loss of weight and a tremendous amount of emotional strain," according to the doctor. Astonishingly, his wife did not visit him; he discharged himself after two days.

Cutting a melancholy figure, Sinatra returns to Los Angeles late in 1953 following hospitalization for complete physical exhaustion.

Amazing, too, was that with a fractured marriage to torment him, Sinatra set about the reconstruction of his career with a zeal that would confound those who considered him dead. But therein lay the artistic nub of Sinatra. In his comeback albums, as in his portrayal of Maggio, he was to pour every vestige of his soul, stepping beyond the dimension of a singer to play … Frank Sinatra. If Frank was able to say of Maggio during his fight to be offered the part: "I *am* that person," he was now able to transmit himself into every vowel and consonant of the *songs* he chose, too.

The elation and the agony he experienced during his partnership with Ava helped build the man we would hear throughout the 1950s and the decades that followed. It caused him to shift from being a vocalist into being an artist.

"Ava Gardner damned near destroyed his career," a Sinatraphile said to me. By causing him to take his eye off the ball of his career, perhaps she was a monumental and dangerous distraction. But, in the context of the period in which Hurricane Ava hit him, her effect was certainly cataclysmic. In Sinatra, however, she brought out the underdog, the fighter, the spirit that needed a cause. He was to convert the experience into a devastating strength. Sinatra was, and is, a battler. Ava was a large part of the fuel he needed to ignite his future artistic stance.

At thirty-six years old, though, Frank had to cast around to reassert himself. A restless spirit, he also had to contend with substantial tax demands. Life could not have seemed too rosy at the start of the 1950s. And yet … if it was possible to detect in his voice the desperation of the loner, Sinatra drew on every vestige of his soul for the decision that would return him to glory. He decided to reinvent himself as Maggio in *From Here to Eternity.*

In retrospect, the movie role of the cheerful underdog who gets beaten up but bounces back seems as if it had been written for him. But acquiring the role did not come easily. Sinatra had lobbied hard for it, beating off competition from more established actors, and reportedly telling the film executives that he would accept a mere $8,000 if they gave him the break. His normal film fees were around $150,000.

Sinatra was making the most spectacular gamble of his life. He plunged into the part, identifying with the hapless soldier so intuitively that fellow actors like Montgomery Clift were mightily impressed. So often, whether singing or acting, Sinatra found that his personality was so powerful that it could never be submerged in favor of anyone or anything. For the first time on the screen, he slipped into the psyche of someone else with a sensitivity that was immensely touching.

In retrospect, it's simplistic to say that Sinatra, dejected as he was from a career on the skids, projected his misery into his depiction of Private Maggio. The reality has a richer truth. Though Sinatra had considerable experience in movies before *Eternity,* no storyline had called upon him to personalize his life before the camera. He knew precisely how to play Maggio, because he was that soldier. Praise was heaped on him by the critics. And he received the ultimate accolade: an Academy Award as best supporting actor.

This was no mere comeback. Stupendous in his chutzpah, skilful in his identification of the part as crucially his own, and brilliant in his execution of it, Sinatra had staged a turnaround that will stand forever as an example of guile and determination in show business.

It was 1953. The talk of the town, Frank Sinatra now held the aces once again … as an actor. All he needed to do now was prove that he wasn't a washed-up singer. His ability wasn't in question, but his record sales were poor. To steer the voice back on track, Sinatra would require a fresh, invigorating, imaginative ally. Such a man would need to be empathetic and revolutionary, fitting Sinatra's audacious style like a glove while refocusing its surrounding sounds.

Frank found him. His name was Nelson Riddle.

From Here to Eternity, directed by Fred Zinneman, provided the startling turnaround in Sinatra's career. He played with dedicated conviction the role of Private Maggio, and fellow actors (some like Burt Lancaster, seen on set above) were mightily impressed. The well-justified Oscar for best supporting actor and actress went to Sinatra and his co-star Donna Reed.

The phenomenon of the pop or rock star had not arrived fully in the year 1953. Wartime swooning for Sinatra had not emerged as a trend; the bloom was off the rose for Sinatra, but no other artist replicated the level of mania he had once commanded. Calmer waters flowed through the entertainment scene. Quality musicianship and vocalists abounded. Tony Bennett scored million-sellers with "Stranger in Paradise" (from the show *Kismet*) and "Rags to Riches." Other million-sellers included Eddie Fisher with "I'm Walking Behind You" and "Oh Mein Papa"; Joni James with the Hank Williams country and western classic "Your Cheatin' Heart"; Dean Martin with "That's Amore"; Patti Page with "That Doggie in the Window" and "Changing Partners"; the pioneering Les Paul and Mary Ford with "Vaya con Dios"; and Jim Reeves with "Mexican Joe." In Britain, light orchestrals were very successful, led by Mantovani and Frank Chacksfield with "Song from Moulin Rouge" and the "Limelight" theme respectively. One of the most popular records on English-speaking radio stations around the world was the million-selling Stan Freberg satire, "St. George and the Dragonet" and "Little Red Riding Hood." But none of these artists aroused any commotion for their personalities.

Unknown to the world, the first rumblings of rock 'n' roll were on the horizon. Bill Haley and his Comets scored with "Crazy Man Crazy," and over the next two years, with "Shake Rattle and Roll" and "Rock Around the Clock," the same group would begin a musical and cultural revolution.

Amid all those million-sellers, it was incredible that Frank Sinatra did not have a record deal. When his contract with Columbia expired at the end of 1952 and the label did not renew, there was a deafening silence from other labels. What an indictment of a record industry that failed to support, encourage and champion artistry of his caliber!

Simultaneously with his activity on the set of *From Here to Eternity*, Frank had to face up to this cold fact: his recording career had reached a nadir. He was one of the finest singers of popular music in history even then, but his temporary silence was of minimal interest to a media more concerned with waspishly recording the details of his domestic strife. Cast by reporters as a swashbuckling, bad-tempered wise guy, Sinatra responded abrasively. A few writers continued to believe in him, but in every compartment of his life this was a solitary period. Paradoxically, this suited him. Driven since birth by a will to make it, Sinatra was not going to be knocked down easily. This extraordinary fight for musical survival would emerge as the backbone of the legend.

After a barren few months, during which he was offered to several record companies, Frank had a new deal. His agency, William Morris, found he had some supporters at what was then a small label, Capitol, and Frank signed into what would be a seven-year relationship … and began one of the most exhilarating stories in popular music.

During the fallow period, rumors persisted that Frank's voice was failing. This was a ploy by writers eager to explain his decline. Though the tension caused by his off-stage life caused him physical stress, the voice never deserted him. He was a natural singer, not one who overloaded his vocal cords, and his use of his voice as a means of expression contrasted with those who strained themselves. Sinatra was about to confound the cynics.

The impetus for his new career came from the colleagues in music whom he chose. Taste, he has always stated, had been the cornerstone in his work all his life. In and out of the recording studio, on the concert trail, he inspired extraordinary loyalty and a reciprocation of his intensity. As he launched himself into the second phase of his recording life, Sinatra was about to experience remarkable chemistry with an unexpected new arranger.

Historically, the man at the baton for Frank had been Axel Stordahl. A talented arranger with the Tommy Dorsey Band when Frank joined it, Stordahl was the "engine room" of the band, highly prized by Dorsey. When Frank left the band, Stordahl went with him, giving him continuity and credibility during those first heady years of life as a soloist. Stordahl conducted the orchestra on all Sinatra's radio shows, notably on the series called *Songs by Sinatra* which reached millions of homes.

At the Capitol label, Voyle Gilmore was designated as Frank's producer. The consensus was that Frank would need to develop a fresh stance to attract a new audience. Although he still had a core following, it would have diminished, and the challenge facing him and Capitol was to reassert the voice in a fresh setting.

Into this cauldron came Nelson Riddle. Taciturn, individualistic and inventive, he had an impeccable pedigree with which to be the man to kick-start Sinatra's career. Importantly, he was from the same neck of the woods as Frank—Riddle had been born six years later than Sinatra, in Oradell, New Jersey—and from the age of eight had been a musician-in-the making, switching from piano to trombone. Turning professional after leaving school, he played trombone and arranged with the bands of Charlie Spivack, Jerry Wald and Tommy Dorsey. On return from wartime service in an Army band, he joined Bob Crosby's band but quickly gave up playing in favor of joining NBC as a staff arranger.

The clincher was that he had worked with Nat King Cole on a string of that great singer's hits, notably "Too Young," "Mona Lisa" and "Somewhere Along the Way."

Awaiting Riddle was a very different artist from Nat Cole, whose relaxed singing style was epitomized by his personality. When I interviewed Cole in London, I found a charming, courteous, gentlemanly figure whose manner seemed the opposite of the image conjured up by the feisty Sinatra in those years. Frank *commanded* his studio work, paying full respect to his arrangers, but involving himself in the minutiae of the recording process more than Nat Cole and, perhaps, more than any singer in his genre. His new musical arranger would have to demonstrate special qualities to wrest the best from his talent.

On 2 April 1953, Frank entered the old Melrose Avenue studio of Capitol in Hollywood to renew his recording career. For this first date, Axel Stordahl was conducting. The result was a creditable performance of "Lean Baby" and "I'm Walking Behind You," which sold well as a single but hardly carried the indefinable edge required to transport Frank back to the heights.

On 30 April, Sinatra went back to cut more sides. He had made a somewhat radical choice of arranger for this session, a young veteran named Billy May, who, as well as playing trumpet, trombone and piano, had seen service as arranger and conductor with several prestigious bands including Charlie Barnet, Glenn Miller, Les Brown and Woody Herman. He had also scored for Bing Crosby and would go on to work with Ella Fitzgerald and Rosemary Clooney, as well as fronting his own band.

May was quite a coup. But as the sessions were about to begin, he said he could not attend since he had a string of touring engagements with his band in Florida. Nelson Riddle moved in that day to score the swinging version of "South of the Border" and "I've Got the World on a String." Inexplicably, May was credited on the record as the arranger on the first-named song. He said, in later years, that he received royalties for it.

The impact of Nelson Riddle was pivotal in restructuring Frank's career. Punchy, swinging brass scores and an irresistible bounce combined to present Sinatra as he had never been heard before. There was a cheekiness and an air of driving confidence, particularly from the haunting brass sections. "South of the Border," a corny song, still sounds lively, forty years on. And the jauntiness of "I've Got the World on a String," lifted skywards by Riddle's energetic verve and Frank's clear exhilaration, made the lyric sound autobiographical.

Sinatra was back. Within days, Sinatra and Riddle had returned to the studio to record the ballad title song from his movie, *From Here to Eternity.* Riddle showed he could simplify arrangements when a song like this, which called for dramatic intensity, came up.

Frank's tender, evocative reading of the lyric was warm, touching, vibrant. His range and power at the climax showed his immersion in both the song and the movie part.

And then the recording axis shifted a further notch in Frank's favor. Something special happened on the night of 9 December. The respected modern jazz composer-arranger Johnny Richards, who worked alongside Stan Kenton, Charlie Barnet and Dizzy Gillepsie, had written a tune called "Young at Heart." It had been rejected by several singers, including Nat King Cole. Another writer, Jimmy Van Heusen, persuaded Frank to give it a shot.

For any artist, there's a special moment in a career, and this song was momentous in reestablishing Sinatra. Everything was right about it. The mood of the song was joyful,

Teamed up with Nelson Riddle, who was pivotal in restructuring his career, Sinatra was off to a new start. "The Voice" was back!

optimistic, but not flippant. The tune was memorable, with a deceptive and poetic continuity. Riddle's lyrical arrangement was light, the strings striking an almost introspective mood. The tune and the score were strong, and the words merged beautifully. Opening slowly, Frank almost said, rather than sang: "Fairy tales can come true, it can happen to you, if you're young at heart … And life gets more exciting with each passing day … And love is either in your heart or on its way. And if you should survive … Look at all you'll derive from being alive." It spoke to the young—simply, powerfully. Frank sang it with a persuasive innocence. Heard now, neither the sentiment nor the melody nor its performance show any age. To the surprise of everyone, the record was a meteoric success. It tore up the best-sellers and ruled the air waves in 1953, selling a million and hitting the number one spot.

Sinatra had now returned from the doldrums with a hit movie and a hit record for what would emerge as a fairy-tale re-entry into the stratosphere of show business. It was not predictable then, but the second phase of his career would far outstrip his first.

During this period of his artistic renaissance, he and Ava were estranged. Their tempestuous relationship caused Frank much anguish, in the view of his friends; his inner soul must have been deeply affected by what his friends called his obsession.

Some Sinatra followers believe that Ava was a negative influence on his career, since their problematic marriage consumed so much "angst time" for Frank. The reverse is true. Sinatra was able to convert human difficulties such as this into his work with a passion that—who knows?—might not have been there without the turmoil. (Ava filed for divorce in 1954 and it became final two years later.)

Two factors emerge from his troubled years with Ava. First, his prodigious output of work. Any of the peccadilloes of his personal life are dwarfed by the sheer extent of activity that came from Sinatra in the 1950s. As a movie star and recording artist, and as a businessman who kept a firm grip on his affairs, he set an awesome schedule. Measured against the standards of any era, his itinerary for those years is extraordinary. Documenting his embattled personal life has always been a favorite occupation of writers. If a similar scrutiny were applied to his work pattern, the world might have had a different vision of Sinatra.

Secondly, the Ava years coincided with a distinct shift in his vocal emphasis. His repertoire of material grew infinitely richer from year to year, but what good would those songs have been to him if he had remained the singer with the Dorsey band? From the moment he changed gear into Capitol Records and gained Nelson Riddle as a partner, something exciting happened to Sinatra. Singing from within himself, he became less a straight singer, more a dream weaver. Whereas before he had been a professional singer, he now assumed the mantle of a unique interpreter. The songs no longer appeared as if they were cherry-picked from a production line, to be sung wonderfully well by a fine singer; they felt as if they had been constructed exclusively for his psyche. Sammy Cahn, his lyricist on many songs in the future, including "Three Coins in the Fountain," put it succinctly: "I don't write a Sinatra song. I write a song. He makes it a Sinatra song."

Was he able to do this partly because of his personal traumas? Musical artists through the ages have been able to convert private grief or handicaps into cathartic, creative milestones. Billie Holiday, the jazz singer who so inspired Frank, sang such songs as "Good Morning Heartache" with a palpably autobiographical touch; her soul was in her work. Building on his natural strengths, Sinatra was now able to infuse songs with his life experiences and emerge as a new singer after the unexpected million-seller "Young at Heart."

As he nudged forty, the years 1954 and 1955 found him extensively involved in movies, in a schedule that might make actors of the future flinch. His roles contrasted from the dramatic to the lightweight. In *Suddenly,* he played a psychopathic would-be assassin of the president of the United States. This piece of acting was well received, and by the time it was reaching the public, Frank had completed another picture, *Not as a Stranger,* playing the role of a doctor alongside such stellar names as Robert Mitchum, Broderick Crawford and Olivia de Havilland.

If *From Here to Eternity* had been his lynchpin, these movies prompted terrific demand for him as a box-office success for a movie world that dominated entertainment in the decades long before the rise of television and video.

His movies poured out. There he was in *Guys and Dolls* and in *The Man with the Golden Arm,* for which many felt he should have earned another Oscar (for which he was nominated). In *The Tender Trap,* he showed strength as a comedian when he played the role of a show-business agent, and the movie spawned his classic soundtrack single, upbeat, joyful, almost a self-characterization in its homily. Sammy Cahn and Jimmy Van Heusen, the gifted songwriting partnership who would write many more hits for Frank, had provided him with the song "The Tender Trap," a substantial hit. Never was a song constructed so perfectly for the singer, and rarely had a singer been so instantly identified with a song as was Frank with this one.

Two more movies were made in that amazing year of 1955: *Johnny Concho,* in which Frank took the title role as an anti-hero, and *High Society,* a deserved box-office winner that also featured Bing Crosby, Louis Armstrong and Grace Kelly as co-stars. This tour-de-force of gaiety remains, for many, a classic memory of the mood of the age. In this upbeat musical, three music giants of the period found their personalities contrasted well.

In *Suddenly* Sinatra played the leader of a trio intending to assassinate the president.

Frank Sinatra's arrival at Capitol was quickly followed by a technological advance crucial to his evolution: the arrival of the long-playing record. Hitherto, the impact of a recording career had been derived from singles. He had prospered from them, but the LP, at first a ten-inch, eight-track creation, would significantly contribute to his exploration and growth. It would enable a mood to be created, with songs following a logical pattern.

Frank chose to draw from his live performance repertoire for his début into the LP world with *Songs for Young Lovers,* which contained such gems as "My Funny Valentine" and "Violets for Your Furs." Nelson Riddle's expertise contributed to what many Sinatra aficionados still consider one of

Frank's finest sets. That same year, 1954, came his second LP, *Swing Easy,* featuring classics like "Just One of Those Things" and "Wrap Your Troubles in Dreams." "All of Me," which Sinatra kicks off a cappella, stands as one of his finest moments, lightly swinging with an acutely sensitive Riddle arrangement. The track is distinctive for Sinatra's relaxed punch, as he swirls and bends the notes. "Can't you see, I'm just a MESS without you/Take my lips, I wanna lose them/Get a piece of these arms/I'll never use them."

The engaging title song of *The Tender Trap* was a perfect vehicle for Sinatra's voice and expression.

The genius of Sinatra was not restricted to upbeat, cheerful escapism. Joining up with Nelson Riddle for an album called *In the Wee Small Hours,* Sinatra exposed raw sentiment through the moroseness of sixteen songs. With surprising candor, Capitol profiled its artist's domestic life as a backdrop for the album: "The chances are high that at some point in life your inner self will be torn apart, your life thrown into despair and your thoughts plunged into an abyss of hopelessness and self pity. An involved relationship ends and the world is transformed into a pit of sad memories and heartache that can be very difficult to climb out of. Frank Sinatra found himself in such a position when he and Ava Gardner separated after five years. It took him over a year to recover, during which time he experienced all the emotions so poignantly and honestly inscribed on this album." The songs were tortuous, despairing, read with immense feeling by Frank, who must have related to the words of "Glad to Be Unhappy," "Mood Indigo," "What Is This Thing Called Love," "Last Night When We Were Young" and "Ill Wind."

The inner man summoned something to profile his own ardor when he sang "When Your Lover Has Gone," indicator of the more introspective balladeer that was to come. Here, with a lush Riddle accompaniment, was born the warm, languorous interpreter that we would listen to for the next forty years. On the same night that side was cut, 17 February 1955, he turned in the song "In the Wee Small Hours of the Morning." "When your lonely heart has learned its lesson … You'd be hers if only she would call … In the wee small hours of the morning … That's the time you miss her most of all."

The passion was electrifying. His solitude was perfectly reflected in the lyric of the Rodgers and Hart beauty "It Never Entered My Mind." *Wee Small Hours* surprised critics

High Society in 1954
(the re-make of *The
Philadelphia Story*)
teamed Sinatra on
film for the first time
with Bing Crosby.
Here Grace Kelly,
playing the Hepburn
role, adjusts on
set while Frank
contemplates the
wee small hours!

and fans, his switch of mood being praised as adventurous. This was one of his finest moments, heralding his future niche as a unique spokesman for lovelorn material, singing for the lonely, the romantic, the desperate.

This defining period would inscribe Sinatra's name in the history books. Because he was musically stepping out from within himself, he would forever be classed by his contemporaries as something beyond a singer. With these sides, and the ones that were soon to follow, Sinatra would join that élite band of artists such as his friends Judy Garland, Sammy Davis Junior, Edith Piaf, and Barbra Streisand, whose greatness stemmed from simply being themselves on stage. That they and Sinatra were vocalists was incidental to the fact that they were artists: the voice was the paintbrush and what reached the canvas was a manifestation of their expression. Till the end of time, the work that Sinatra began in the mid-1950s, and would go on to execute, would render his name immortal to every generation that cares to study his art.

Rock 'n' roll arrived in 1955. The rumblings had been there for two years, but Bill Haley's record, "Rock Around the Clock," from the film *Blackboard Jungle,* marked a sociological, as well as musical, change. (Sinatra, whose views on the new sound were scarcely printable, would recoil from having it described as music.)

Straight popular music survived. There was balladeer Tennessee Ernie Ford with "Sixteen Tons," the Four Aces with "Love Is a Many Splendored Thing," and soothsayers like Pat Boone, Doris Day and Guy Mitchell. Dean Martin, soon to be Sinatra's lifelong friend, was making his mark with a lilting ballad, "Memories Are Made of This." In Britain, Alma Cogan sang "Dreamboat," Ruby Murray sang "Softly, Softly," Anne Shelton sang "Lay Down Your Arms" and Jimmy Young, later to emerge as a successful broadcaster, sang "The Man from Laramie."

As Bill Haley and his Comets thundered around the cinema stages of Britain, the generation gap was established overnight. Elvis Presley was on course to his legendary status (in 1956 he would score hits with "Don't Be Cruel," "Heartbreak Hotel" and "Love Me Tender"). On the world stage, the US re-elected President Eisenhower, while in Britain Sir Winston Churchill resigned, to be succeeded by Sir Anthony Eden.

In the movie world, James Dean's performance in *Rebel Without a Cause* and Marlon Brando in *The Wild Ones* represented youthful rebellion. Teenagers wanted a new music, and it needed to be as assertive as they were to contrast with the lovey-dovey safety of the ballads their parents had endorsed. The avalanche came thick and fast, Little Richard, Fats Domino, Chuck Berry and Gene Vincent among those spearheading the first attack.

Sinatra's progress was not derailed by the rock 'n' roll trend. As Bill Haley hit the top of the Billboard Hot Hundred charts with "Rock Around the Clock," Frank was at number three in 1955 with "Learnin' the Blues," a robust, mid-tempo song with a neat lyric suited to him: "When you're at home alone the blues will taunt you constantly … When you're out in a crowd, the blues will haunt your memory."

The pleasing track demonstrated the versatility of Nelson Riddle's arrangements, the brass an urgent backdrop to Sinatra's suitably brash delivery. He oozed confidence on this track and tracks that followed that year: from the pen of lyricist Sammy Cahn and his music partner Jimmy Van Heusen, Frank grasped "Love and Marriage," an innocuous hit. The year ended with him again winning music magazine polls as top male singer.

In 1956, a year in which Frank's mentor Tommy Dorsey died, came the landmark album called *Songs for Swingin' Lovers.* A huge seller, it was a "concept album" of its time. There he is on the cover, smiling knowingly, fedora cheekily askance, as a young couple beneath him embrace. The album's notes underscored the theme that another Sinatra-Riddle collaboration would explore in the music.

"For Teenagers," exclaimed Capitol Records about the brave new album. "When he himself was young and frail, Frankie stood in the theatre spotlight and sang with all his heart, till the throng of girls screeched their delight. For adventure-loving moviegoers, he became the ill-starred soldier, Private Maggio, and his spirited, sensitive performance won a coveted Academy Award. For sad romantics, singing bittersweet ballads, he gently caught the mood of the wee small hours of the morning and created a best selling record album. For observers of the social scene he courageously fashioned a new identity in his taut, dramatic film portrayal of the man with the golden arm.

"And now, for swingin' lovers, he returns to what is, after all, home ground … to the happy task of singing the most enchantedly romantic songs he knows. No one can do this with greater verve or skill than can Frank Sinatra, who is surely one of the most knowing and compelling entertainers anywhere."

The marketing of the album, towards a generation of young lovers, was shrewd, the selection of songs beguiling. By now, the best songs in the world were available to Sinatra and he displayed an unerring choice of material correct for his mood, timbre, and personality. He was always totally involved in the pacing of the albums, too, ensuring that song by song there was a logical sequence.

Songs for Swingin' Lovers began with "You Make Me Feel So Young" and seemed to race through songs that move ahead naturally in style and mood, the Riddle scores beefy yet understated. "It Happened in Monterey" and "You're Getting to Be a Habit with Me" came before such classics as "Old Devil Moon" and "Pennies from Heaven"; the Gershwin brothers' "Love Is Here to Stay" closed the first side with Frank's panache, and then came Cole Porter's "I've Got You Under My Skin" to kick off side two.

Frank was recording the album in the Capitol Tower on Vine Street, Hollywood, scene of so many of his future sessions. Who could guess that, forty years after recording that song, U2's Bono would be duetting with him on it?

Beautiful songs sizzled on this collection, from Jimmy Van Heusen and Johnny Mercer's "I Thought About You" to "Swingin' Down the Lane," Cole Porter's "Anything Goes" and "How About You?" It remains the essential example of Sinatra at his most buoyant, and the jazz-inflected, understated accompaniments, with Nelson Riddle at the helm, provided an immaculate backdrop. The album scored a direct hit on the emotions of millions of young lovers. Driven though he was by his youthful exuberance, Sinatra owed much to the flawless arrangements by Nelson Riddle, who later named it as their best recording together.

Anyone who was around Frank Sinatra spoke of his mercurial temperament, his magnetism, his meticulous attitude to his work, and his short fuse. Social friends and professional colleagues testified to his unpredictability. Whether in a restaurant or a recording studio, he put his company on its mettle with those piercing blue eyes, missing nothing.

After 1953, working closely with arrangers Nelson Riddle, Billy May and Gordon Jenkins, Sinatra had turned the recording studio into his theater. His performances were viewed by select groups of close friends, who included here Lauren Bacall and Sophia Loren.

Nelson Riddle considered him "canny." Years of working with more passive performers ranging from Bing Crosby to Ella Fitzgerald had not equipped him to deal with the Sinatra stance, but in their musical symbiosis there was true rapport. Always well prepared for the sessions, which ran from around 8 p.m. until 11 p.m., Sinatra would usually complete about four numbers each night, with an average of three takes per number. Riddle recalled that Sinatra had precise ideas about how the arrangements should be approached, particularly the mood that should be struck at various moments, from loud or soft to happy or sad. Such precision work on albums he had learned from Tommy Dorsey.

Riddle's technique included a surprise element that he once described. He attempted to avoid scoring a song with a climax predictably at the end. He felt it was better to build it midway through a song, or slightly later, enabling the ending to surprise.

In Sinatra, Riddle found a scientific approach to album-making that was unusual for a singer; many of the finest singers were content to leave the planning and execution of the record to the producer and arranger, confining themselves to singing. But Sinatra immersed himself in the entirety of the record, from the selection of songs, whittling down perhaps sixty to a dozen, and then pacing the theme of the collection, deciding on song sequence. As so often happens with the creative process, what looks casual actually stems from scrupulous attention to detail.

Capitol Records stated, in the notes to one album collection, that from 1941 until 1946 Sinatra was said to have earned about $11 million. "But from 1953 through 1960, The Great Years, Sinatra grossed more than $30 million, if his earnings from records, motion pictures, television, radio and certain other sources and investments are totalled."

It wasn't, however, a hunger for money that motivated him from the mid-1950s onwards. It was an abiding love for making records, which gave him more pleasure than any other facet of his activity.

The trend continued at his own Reprise label. Seen here with Frank Junior in the background learning some tricks.

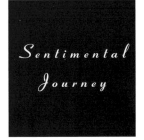

Sentimental Journey

The mythology of Sinatra, inextricably linked to his personality as well as to his music, cast him as a battler. This worked well for him. News of his combat with journalists spanned the globe and, while some experiences were pugnacious, he usually protested that any encounter was in the name of fair play. His well-documented views of reporters were that they too often paraded lies about him and that his private life should remain just that.

He was prickly, too, when faced by hecklers on his live appearances. And if his tongue lacerated, he also displayed a droll, if cruel, sense of humor. Outside his bachelor house in Coldwater Canyon hung a sign: "If you haven't been invited, you'd better have a damn good reason for ringing this bell."

In his element and his natural habitat— Vegas and The Sands Hotel, 1960—the renaissance was in full swing.

Frank's homes, one in Coldwater Canyon and another in New York with a magnificent view of the East River, were described by singer Marion Ryan, mother of singers Paul and Barry Ryan. She gushed, "In my book, Frank is a number one guy, both as a person and a host. I was so overcome when I met the great man with friends, I was struck absolutely dumb, just like a young fan, in fact! He asked what I wanted to drink. I managed to stutter out: 'I'll have what you are having.' The laugh was on me, for I ended up with a huge beer."

Frank's home life was, Marion said, "absolutely fabulous. His home or apartment looks as though it has been designed for a lavish film set. It's all in exquisite taste. The first thing that struck me, though, is that Frank's homes are essentially bachelor places. Everything is clean cut. The décor is bright and he favors orange, black, gold and cinnamon brown shades. There's a very Oriental touch about his furniture and ornaments. He likes Chinese black lacquer and gold tables, all very low. And the bathrooms, particularly, are very exotic." The taps were shaped like swans, with gold and black stools dotted around.

At the time of his clashes with the media, his image suffered; his brashness was considered ugly. But it came with the package of the man, and if at times he crossed the line into poor taste in public behavior, we must ask if a different person would have produced the same music. Away from the spotlight, Sinatra railed against perceived injustice, played out his romances in the full glare of publicity, and at the same time amassed a huge circle of supporters.

With kindred spirits who dominated their era in show business, he instigated two separate private members' clubs whose aims and ground rules were blurred. The first, the Rat Pack, in the mid 1950s, had as its members Frank's friends Humphrey Bogart, Judy Garland and Lauren Bacall. When Bogart died on 14 January 1957, this precipitated the formation of a new show business group that would run into the 1960s: the Clan featured Frank alongside Sammy Davis Junior, Dean Martin and Peter Lawford.

Leaders of the pack, or the Clan. Here Dean Martin, Sammy Davis Junior and Sinatra celebrate following their performance at a fund-raiser at Carnegie Hall for Martin Luther King Junior in 1961.

If the function of these two "organizations," besides enjoying hedonism, was foggy, they told us that, beyond the headlines, Sinatra enjoyed a wide network of friends who swore allegiance to him, and not because of his power and talent. While his image in the media sometimes took a beating, reporters, even if they wanted to, were unable to dent his love affair with his public. From the moment he was able to reverse his fortune, his status did not endure, it grew. He needed his friends, and he cherished them. Sinatra's legendary short fuse was neatly summarized by his friend Vincente Minnelli, former husband of Judy Garland and father of Liza.

Minnelli, who directed the film in which Frank starred called *Some Came Running,* wrote in his autobiography, *I Remember It Well:* "Sinatra is feisty as a rooster, and if you don't think that adequately describes the towering rages of which he's capable, have you ever seen a cockfight?

"Once his friend, you're a friend for life. He's the greatest foul weather friend, and in this up and down business, Frank has meant constancy to so many during the bad times. Of course, he's prone to tell friends how he'll help them rather than ask how he can help. But I suppose that's the prerogative of any leader of the Clan."

Minnelli continued that when Frank did render assistance, it was beyond discussion. He recalls how, when he wanted to use a song in a picture, and he was having difficulties, Frank was away in the Orient. Minnelli phoned him. "Don't worry," Sinatra told him. "It's yours." Minnelli thanked him, asking for clarification, "But how…" Sinatra interrupted Minnelli, enunciating each of the following words: "It is yours." Adds Minnelli: "I wasn't on the phone with him for more than three minutes but before I'd hung up the cogs had already started moving to get permission to use the song."

Contrasting with the criticism of his off-stage persona, he inspired fierce loyalty for his unswerving support and gestures of largese. Peggy Lee, recalling in her book Frank's involvement in one of her albums, *The Man I Love,* remembers how delighted she was when she learned he was building a house near hers in California. His friend forever after the kindnesses he had showed her back at the Paramount Theatre, Peggy said: "There have been very few men in our business who have affected me so deeply I can't express myself, and Frank is one of them. . . . Frank invited me to his house so many times for dinners or parties or movies in his theatre." They shared quiet talks, funny jokes, and *The Man I Love* album was "totally his concept." Frank took Peggy a long list of songs from which to choose and Bill

Miller, Frank's pianist, went over to see her to set all the keys. Then Frank hired Nelson Riddle, says Peggy, "to write those lovely arrangements as Frank conducted them, a marvellously sensitive conductor as one would expect." An insight into Frank's total immersion in a project came from Peggy Lee when she revealed that Frank even designed and supervised the cover. "He is a producer who thinks of everything, even putting menthol in my eyes so I'd have a misty look in the cover photograph. Frank Sinatra has always been somewhere near, just touching the elbow, holding the hand. . . ."

Later, Peggy Lee reveals in her autobiography how, when she was in hospital in New Orleans, Frank called her many times. "He gave me strength and kept urging me to get well: 'We've got to get you home, baby.'" When finally she could leave for her California home, he sent a private plane to fly her with her nurse, assistant and daughter back to the West Coast.

Regularly and quietly, Sinatra paid hospital bills for friends, made his private plane available to them, and on hundreds of occasions, touchingly and unexpectedly, dispensed all manner of practical and psychological support to his extended family. He rushed to the aid of Sammy Davis when he was involved in an horrific car crash. And in two cases at least, Sinatra's philanthropic hand was extended to artists with whom he had survived brushes to become friends: comedian Joe E. Lewis and Buddy Rich, his former *bête noir* in the Dorsey band. When Rich wanted to go solo, Sinatra, recognizing a master drummer, funded his foray into bandleading.

There were signals, too, of the philanthropist whom we came to recognize later. In the mid-1950s, he spoke about his wish to stage shows in capital cities around the world to benefit underprivileged children. This plan came true about five years later.

Whether these activities were examples of one man's need to be loved (in itself no crime), they confirmed him as flesh and blood.

And he always looked snazzy. Sinatra always displayed an air of cultivated smartness. He was never seen with scuffed shoes, unkempt casuals, or in anything less than understated classy garb. Nor was this something that came especially with riches; right back to his days with the James and Dorsey bands, colleagues recall his fastidiousness and the fact that he kept hotel valets busy (and generously tipped) the length and breadth of the US. Back in Hoboken, as a teenager, he had been nicknamed Slacksy, so often did he buy new trousers.

A rebel he may have been in adulthood, but from his youth he was of his era. The teenage battling kid of Hoboken had no bearing on his demeanor, always neat and respectful. "He was pushy but polite," said one music business colleague.

Rock 'n' roll seemed the antithesis of everything Frank Sinatra stood for, as a man and as an artist. The self-discipline, the ground rules in music, and the craftsmanship of the songwriters for whom he had been a flagship were threatened by the arrival of Presley, Bill Haley, Jerry Lee Lewis, and Little Richard. Examined today, his remarks on the subject seem reactionary, but the disgust at the arrival of "devil's music" hit Sinatra deeply.

Deploring Elvis and the revolution of the young, Sinatra said that he had "deep sorrow" for the "unrelenting insistence of recording and motion picture companies upon purveying the most brutal, ugly, degenerate, vicious form of expression it has been my displeasure to hear and naturally I'm referring to the bulk of rock 'n' roll."

He went on to charge that it brought about "almost totally negative and destructive reactions in young people. It smells phoney and false. It is sung, played and written for the most part by cretinous goons and by means of its almost imbecilic reiterations and sly, lewd, in plain fact dirty, lyrics, it manages to be the martial music of every sideburned delinquent on earth." His wrath was understandable. He sang about love and romance. Many rockers sang about sex.

What divided Frank and his generation from rock 'n' roll was something far beyond music. When Dorsey and Riddle *et al.* played and he sang, it was great music, pure and simple. It carried no sociological overtones. The bobbysoxers who had dubbed him King of Swoon saw him simply as an idol; they did not look to him for a new lifestyle, or for a key to any attitude they should be adopting. There was nothing subversive about standing before a microphone, exploring relationships between man and woman. Rock 'n' roll changed all that. Carrying with it a mode of dress, outlook, and tilting against authority, the new sounds came upon us with a vigorous war cry. The world, and the music map, would never be the same. While Frank stood as the beacon of evergreen popular music, the young had a new language all their own.

In Liverpool, England, during the summer of 1957, Paul McCartney met John Lennon for the first time at a church garden party. The teenagers would soon go on to form the Beatles, shifting the axis in popular music from America for the first time.

In Hollywood's Capitol Tower at that same time, Frank Sinatra was launching yet another phase in his career. Again, he was to be partnered by a new conductor-arranger who would help him break exciting new ground.

Gordon Jenkins came to the side of Sinatra with a remarkable history. Five years older than Frank, he had been the pianist-arranger in the early 1930s with the highly popular Isham Jones Band. He later arranged, gaining plaudits for the originality of his scores, for Paul Whiteman and Benny Goodman, for whom he composed that band's closing theme, "Goodbye." He worked with Artie Shaw, Louis Armstrong, Peggy Lee, Judy Garland and Nat King Cole as well as leading his own lush orchestra.

As they entered the studio to record together in April and May 1957, another important technological step was to hand: their forthcoming album would be Frank's first in the exciting new sound known as stereo.

Jenkins, who wrote "This Is All I Ask," one of the finest compositions in popular music, was a gentle, quiet man. Sinatra described him as a "softie," whom he adored. His music mirrored his character. It was rich, string-laden and deep.

"Gordon displayed sensitivity. When you spoke to him, you felt it. You heard it. I was crazy about his orchestrations," Sinatra recalled. The songs recorded for their first album together testify to Sinatra's words.

Yet another groundbreaker, the album called *Where Are You?* was like nothing Sinatra had done. Following a more traditional Sinatra album called *A Swinging Affair,* the Jenkins partnership yielded an intensely personal collection that focused on loneliness and yearning. On "Autumn Leaves," "Laura," "The Night We Called It a Day" and the haunting title track, Frank got inside the lyrics with rare insights into the human condition. The arrangements by Jenkins were imaginative, a perfection of intimate mood creations. As for the song "Laura"… Sinatra singing that must have touched millions of girls with that name. There was even the song partly written by Sinatra, the creditable "I'm a Fool to Want You."

Contrasting with the more predictable swing of Billy May on songs like "Come Fly with Me," this album with Gordon Jenkins would be, for students of Sinatra through the years, a cornerstone of his work. It was Frank's first major evidence of his ability to transmit

Pal Joey **teamed Sinatra with Rita Hayworth and Kim Novak, and provided him with the definitive "The Lady is a Tramp."**

heartful tenderness into lyrics. Mood albums like *In the Wee Small Hours* had been good, but Jenkins somehow brought out more depth in the singer. As their partnership progressed, they were to record an all-time classic, *The Sinatra Christmas Album*, featuring seasonal favorites like "Have Yourself a Merry Little Christmas," "Silent Night," "The Christmas Song"… and another song part-written by Frank, "Mistletoe and Holly."

Sammy Davis observed that in Frank's stage show, it was not just women who adored his combination of vulnerability and tough guy. Men admired him because he had fought the odds and won, and also because many secretly considered him a role model.

As rock 'n' roll strengthened its grip on the young, Sinatra seemed, from 1957 until the end of the decade, to mark time as a recording artist. The reasons would emerge clearly later, but his movie activity in those years seemed to take priority over his records. He played opposite Rita Hayworth in *Pal Joey*. In this adaptation of the last Rodgers and Hart musical, Frank took the role of a small-time heel who, through the patronage of a rich woman, becomes the proprietor of a nightclub. Set in San Francisco, the movie has Frank singing some notable tracks, including "Bewitched, Bothered and Bewildered," "The Lady Is a Tramp," "I Didn't Know What Time It Was" and "There's a Small Hotel."

He took the part of a Spanish revolutionary in *The Pride and the Passion*. The cheerful song "High Hopes," always to be a radio favorite, came from the movie *A Hole in the Head,* in which Frank played opposite Edward G. Robinson. Written by Sammy Cahn and Jimmy Van Heusen, the song was bright enough but by now there was a general feeling that Frank was singing formula songs rather predictably.

When he found great songs, of course, he homed in on them. Two compositions, "All the Way" and "Chicago," which became Frank's sixth million-seller in 1957, both came from *The Joker is Wild.* In this movie, Frank played the role of a nightclub singer in the twenties whose career is halted by a gangland attack in which his vocal cords are slashed. "All the Way," which was written by Cahn and Van Heusen and won an Academy Award as best film song of the year, was a beauty, the title and the storyline seemingly the embodiment of the singer's make-up. As for "Chicago"… it was an oldie from 1922, written by Fred Fisher and a million-seller in sheet music in that year.

Opposite Edward G.Robinson in *A Hole in the Head*, directed by Frank Capra. The film produced an Oscar for the song "High Hopes" by Sammy Cahn.

With the intrusion, as Frank saw it, of rock 'n' rollers, 1957 was a very competitive year, when singers of his style had to compete for record sales with new names. Younger artists who made their mark with million-sellers that would be played till the end of time were Paul Anka ("Diana"), Sam Cooke ("You Send Me"), the Everly Brothers ("Bye Bye Love"), Buddy Holly ("Peggy Sue" and "Every Day"), and Jerry Lee Lewis, Elvis Presley and Fats Domino. The music scene was changing, and while it was inconceivable that Sinatra should alter his style, he had been in the game of making music for long enough to know he should be reappraising his situation.

At Capitol, his producer changed in 1958. Voyle Gilmore was succeeded by Dave Cavanaugh, and with Nelson Riddle's baton, another hallmark album was created. *Only the Lonely* carried a masterly version of "Blues in the Night." The barroom theme of the album suited Sinatra in every conceivable way, and for the song that was indelibly associated with him there were two fascinating studio "effects." In club and concert dates, Sinatra sang "One for My Baby (and One More for the Road)" just before intermission. With the house lights invariably out, smoking a cigarette whose smoke circled upwards through a solitary spotlight, Sinatra leaned on the piano of his pianist Bill Miller and played the role of the maudlin drunk. The song speaks, rather than sings, his despair eloquently: he's afraid to face the night and go home because there's no one to go home to. He turned away from the microphone and walked away in the last chorus, so that his final words were barely audible, a theatrical gesture applauded by an audience recognizing the sadness of the story.

In the recording studio Cavanaugh brilliantly simulated the atmosphere of a Sinatra live performance, dimming the lights so that a solitary spotlight picked out the singer. And instead of having any orchestral backing, the accompaniment consisted of just a tinkling piano. It was a master touch. "It's quarter to three/there's no one in the place except you and me …" sang Frank, and from the pen of Harold Arlen and Johnny Mercer came certainly one of the top songs ever to be associated with Sinatra. He always sang songs of aching despair from the heart as well as from the head. "One for My Baby" remains a signature Sinatra classic; small wonder that when the song came to be re-recorded in 1992, there could be no vocal accompanist. The role of instrumentalist went to the soulful and tasteful contemporary soprano saxophonist Kenny G.

The song stands as compelling evidence of Sinatra's assumption of the role of actor-singer. The album on which it starred, *Only the Lonely,* reached number two on the best-selling chart, knocked off its perch by *Come Fly with Me.* This, though it featured the kick of Billy May and some notable songs like "Moonlight in Vermont," "Autumn in New York," "Let's Get Away from It All" and "It's Nice to Go Travelling," was a fairly predictable piece of work.

If, with hindsight, he was treading water a little in the latter part of the 1950s, it was dangerous to underestimate the man. If he was not pushing forward, the defensive question was: why should he? With the body of work he had already established, he was entitled to go on an artistic "hold"; many artists took time off to reflect after an infinitely smaller volume of work.

In reality, he did not opt out. He failed to surprise us with the tempo of his work (more movies, more hits) but it was fundamentally more of the same. Here he was again with the movie *Can Can,* with Shirley MacLaine as his co-star and also Maurice Chevalier … and Juliet Prowse as a dancer. The musical, set in Paris, featured Frank singing "It's All Right with Me," "Let's Do It" and, of course, "I Love Paris." He was the most in-demand actor in show business. Where was the surprise factor?

It came in March and May, 1959—not from a movie but, thankfully, in the shape of a new album. With Gordon Jenkins, he returned to the Capitol Tower to cut a dozen tracks in pensive mood. The album was to be called *No One Cares.*

The legend of Sinatra is not built upon his young, rakish personality or his thespian abilities or his aptitude for film comedy, or the personal edginess of his later years. It is not built upon his sparring with the world's press or his romantic affiliations. It is surely based on our innate feeling that here is a man who can speak from his heart about our own.

To this writer, *No One Cares* was the best album he ever made because it went places that no other singer could possibly go. It created the mood of the title perfectly, and the instigation and delivery of that message was entirely Sinatra's work.

Responding to the melancholic tone set by Gordon Jenkins's scores, Sinatra personally structured the album from song to song, and set the running order. Explaining the pacing of the album to author Robin Douglas-Home in 1962, Sinatra said he wrote the titles of the songs on twelve bits of paper and juggled them like a jigsaw until the album told a complete story, lyric-wise. "For example, the album is in the mood of 'No One Cares'—track one. Why does no one care? Because there's 'A Cottage for Sale'—track two. That song's the saddest song ever written, by the way. It depicts the complete breakup of a home. So on right through to the last track, which might be 'One for My Baby and One More for the Road'—the end of the episode." Sinatra added that he learned such precision programming from Tommy Dorsey's itinerary for the band concerts.

"Stormy Weather" was sung with a richness and full voice of considerable power. Side One concluded with the resignation of "I Don't Stand a Ghost of a Chance with You" before closing with "Here's That Rainy Day." Written by Johnny Burke and Jimmy Van Heusen, the song is pure poetry. He invests the song with poignant beauty, and with his natural pauses and timing, plus Jenkins's skilful work with the strings, it stands as certainly among his greatest recorded tracks. It is, reportedly, the favorite song of Frank's wife Barbara, who shows innate taste in choosing it. It was an album evoking a mood of despair. Sinatra's life, with its roller-coaster moments, had provided him with all the insights he needed for material like this.

Sinatra became a friend and confidant of John F. Kennedy when he ran for the Presidency in 1960.

Side Two began with "I Can't Get Started," the jazz standard, and he gave it the same element of hopelessness that made the classic trumpet version by Bunny Berigan a definitive reading. Each track vied with the last for soulfulness. "Just Friends" went into "I'll Never Smile Again" and "None but the Lonely Heart," Sinatra bathed in pathos. On a set of despondent lyrics that called for naked involvement, Sinatra gave something from within himself on *No One Cares.* Topping its nearest album competitors, *Where Are You?* and *In the Wee Small Hours,* it presented Sinatra at the apogee of his genius ... as an artist alone. As the American commentator on music Ralph J. Gleason wrote in his notes to the album, Sinatra possessed "that degree of personal magnetism discernible only in artists who have risen so far above the ordinary that they are able to do automatically what many good artists can do only occasionally."

No One Cares, a triumph, found Frank disconsolate in its musical setting. By coincidence, it matched his mood about his life inside his record company.

Capitol had been a haven to him since 1953. But for a year or so, Frank had been restless. Always fascinated by the machinery of show business, he wanted to run his own

show. When he went to Capitol to ask for a release, they insisted he cut four albums to wind up his association with them and complete the contract.

Those were the strictures under which his final records with Capitol were made. It speaks volumes for his own dedication to his work that, with records of the quality of *No One Cares* among the final cuts, he would never pawn his standards even when his back was against the wall.

Shortly after Frank left Capitol, Alan Livingston, who had been instrumental in signing him to the label and was the label's vice-president of creative services, stated that the records being released by the industry at that time, including those by his own company, comprised "a wasteland composed of unneeded, unwanted, unworthy discs." Describing "a flood of substandard products that could choke the industry to death," he condemned the lack of creativity, adding: "The ratio of best-selling albums to total output is one in twenty-two. The implication is clear: we are making too many records, worthless records, bad records."

That could not have been a condemnation of Sinatra, whose standards never faltered. But if it reflected an atmosphere inside Capitol, he would have been quick to spot it.

In September 1961, Frank recorded his final album for Capitol, supported by his old friend Axel Stordahl and the orchestra. Provocatively entitled *Point of No Return,* this showed no sign of the tension that must have been within him outside the studio. Behind the microphone, he was, as ever, the consummate professional and his readings of classy songs, "As Time Goes By," "Somewhere Along the Way," "Memories of You," "September Song" and "These Foolish Things," formed a fitting valediction.

By then he had already recorded his début work for his own new label, in studio sessions that straddled his forty-fifth birthday in December 1960. "Now … a newer,

At the presidential inaugural gala, Sinatra was responsible for the entertainers who, here in rehearsal, included: Nat King Cole, Harry Belafonte, Kay Thompson, Jimmy Durante, Helen Traubel, Sammy Cahn, Allan King, Gene Kelly, Janet Leigh, Peter Lawford, and Milton Berle. JFK announced, "We are all indebted to a great friend, Frank Sinatra. Tonight we have seen excellence."

happier, emancipated Sinatra," trumpeted the new label, which he called Reprise. "Untrammelled, unfettered, unconfined. On Reprise." It was a barely concealed "Yippee, I'm free" message to his old company.

After some legal wrangles with his old label, Sinatra displayed all the "hands-on" technique for which he was famous, in every corner of his life, rapidly establishing Reprise as a successful home for talent. Ten years later, the rock generation would be making a lot of noise about the launch of artist-owned labels; but Sinatra did it first. Reprise was launched under the financial and administrative wing of Warner Brothers.

The setting up of the Reprise operation stemmed from his strong interest in the organizational and financial aspect of the industry. Bearing the imprimatur of Sinatra, and even his photograph on the records, Reprise featured initially Sammy Davis Junior, Dean Martin, the Hi-Los vocal group, satirist Mort Sahl, jazz singer Jimmy Witherspoon, jazz saxophonist Ben Webster, and Frank's daughter, singer Nancy, who was by then married to singer Tommy Sands.

In *The Manchurian Candidate* John Frankenheimer directed Sinatra in one of his best roles. He uncovers the plot by a brainwashed fellow-captive of the Koreans to assassinate the President.

In listening anew to the début album made by Sinatra for Reprise, the buoyancy and different mood struck by the singer become clear. The album was called *Ring-a-Ding Ding!,* a theme pursued by the new label, and the eponymous song, by Cahn and Van Heusen, sounded as if it was being performed by a new singer trying to establish himself—which, in a real sense, Sinatra was trying to do. The confidence was boosted by lively arrangements by the arranger chosen by Sinatra, Johnny Mandel, formerly a trombonist with the Count Basie Band. Sinatra strode through some classics like "Let's Face the Music," "I've Got My Love to Keep Me Warm," and "The Coffee Song" with a verve we hadn't heard in his final Capitol records.

His industriousness on the movie front continued with *Sergeants Three,* a poor, cliché-ridden movie that featured his pals Dean Martin, Sammy Davis Junior and Peter Lawford. It was not well received by the press. By contrast, *The Manchurian Candidate,* a thriller of which Frank was justly proud, was hailed as displaying Sinatra at his best once again. One of his strongest movies, it cast him as a captive in Korea, and Sinatra assumed a demanding role with great conviction.

But the decade was not going to bring another diet of records and films alone. He was to become active in humanitarian causes and assume the mantle of a king of charity. There was nothing particularly new, or surprising, about the way he plunged into a journey around the world to aid underprivileged children in 1962. He had been consistent in his work for tolerance and fair play and now he was in a position to channel his energy and popularity into active service.

In previous years, Sinatra had worked for the Polio Drive, National Brotherhood Week observation sponsored by the Conference of Christians and Jews, and the Heart Fund. In 1961 and 1962 he went to Mexico City to perform on behalf of the National Rehabilitation Institute and also to Acapulco to help a children's hospital. His charitable works for children spread throughout the world, and in April 1962 he embarked on a world tour. From Tokyo to Hong Kong, from Israel to Athens, from Rome on to Milan, Paris and London, this was an entertainer enjoying the wielding of his gigantic influence. The aim was to raise a million dollars in total, a figure that was exceeded wildly.

An orphanage was named after him in Hong Kong. In Israel, an Interfaith Youth Center was built in Nazareth and named after him. In Tokyo he presented one million yen to an orphanage. All tour expenses were paid by Sinatra, including musicians, staff and equipment.

What was the world to deduce from this huge operation? Clearly, Sinatra would spread material warmth and caring to children and the adults who worked with them. The tour would produce funds and generate compassion as a colossus of the entertainment world gave various charities his blessing. But what did Sinatra's decision to do a marathon world charity tour tell us about the man?

Nobody scales the peaks like Sinatra did without crossing swords. In some quarters he was considered a parvenu, and his public tantrums with reporters, together with his known impatience, rightly gave him a reputation for rudeness at best. It is impossible, though, to judge the man separately from the artist. Who but a soulful spirit could imbue the lyrics to a song like "Last Night When We Were Young," that majestic beauty by Harold Arlen and Yip Harburg, with such pathos? Who but a deeply sentimental person could read such feeling into the Rodgers and Hart song "It Never Entered My Mind?" Who but one who cared could inject such strength into Alex Wilder's simplistic "I'll Be Around" as Sinatra did?

There have been deeper forces at work in Sinatra's psyche than were evident from the more superficial aspect of the man's public face. From the 1960s on, his image softened until, three decades on, he was seen as a great singer rather than a difficult fellow.

The world charity tour of 1962 seemed an affirmation, too, that having scaled the heights and made his fortune, Sinatra had never wanted to forget who he was, nor ignore the roots of his Hoboken childhood. There was nothing corny or maudlin about his wish to be the philanthropic troubadour, repaying in his way the fruits of his success.

His concerts in London as part of this journey began on 1 June 1962 at the Royal Festival Hall, London, at a concert attended by Princess Margaret and a veritable galaxy of stars. Like many performers, Sinatra was hugely impressed with the acoustics of the hall and gave what is generally considered one of the best shows of his career to that date. London was special to him, and it showed. Surprisingly, in the light of his impact on Britain through his records and films, this was Sinatra's first appearance in the country since his UK and European tour nine years earlier.

I saw his concert, which was among three London shows, at the Gaumont (now Apollo), Hammersmith, on 3 June. The charities to benefit were the Sunshine Fund for Blind Babies and Children and the National Society for Mentally Handicapped Children.

Putting great energy into charity, Sinatra visited a nursing home in Paris for the treatment of crippled boys. His World Charity Tour of 1962 raised a million or more dollars for children.

The atmosphere was electric as John Dankworth and his orchestra with Cleo Laine, followed by the Don Riddell Four, opened the show. After the intermission, Sinatra strode out to tumultuous applause before launching into his repertoire with vigor. He was accompanied by a sextet led by his pianist Bill Miller, who had joined Sinatra in 1951 and whose name would become irrevocably linked as his musical associate through to the present day. As with all those who stood alongside Sinatra, Miller's credentials were impeccable: he had come through the respected bands of Charlie Barnet and Red Norvo in the 1930s and 1940s when he joined the Jimmy Dorsey Band. At Frank's side for some of the Capitol work and in his "crossover" to the launch of Reprise, Miller displayed a telepathic musical communication with Sinatra and was to consolidate his reputation as his crucial pianist as the years passed.

That night at Hammersmith was the first time I had seen Sinatra perform, although I had been collecting his records since *Young at Heart* had gripped me in 1953. His songs touched every mood, from the tenderness of "Imagination" through to the drive of "Come Fly with Me." It was a majestic concert, not a note out of place. But there was something more than just good songs, uniquely sung. There is something electric about Sinatra's stage persona; he occupies the stage with dignity and you just know, from the start, that here is an artist dedicated to perfection. The songs are classics, the musicianship he demands is clearly in the top division.

A year before coming to London for these shows, Sinatra had become a friend and confidante of America's new president, John F. Kennedy, and had staged his inaugural gala. At the start of the decade, therefore, Sinatra had an aura that went beyond the entertainment world. Sammy Davis Junior, whom I interviewed in London at that time, told me: "Sinatra is lucky. He can create a mood any time. He just has to play himself. I'm different. I have to work on establishing a mood. Frank is … well, he's on his own." When asked about the Clan, he reacted strongly, defensively: "The whole business bores me. There is no Clan. I am totally fed up with the word. Somebody started talking about a group of friends in that way, and it's time it was ended. I've got close friends like anybody else, and Frank and Dean Martin are among them. That's all. The only clan I know about is in Scotland."

Frank Sinatra's British concerts were presented by his European representative, the impresario Harold Davison, who formed a friendship with the star and gave his impressions of the man behind the public image during an interview in the *Melody Maker* at that time. Visiting Frank on the set of the movie *Come Blow Your Horn,* Davison reported: "That guy is really a perfectionist. He'll go over a scene again and again until he gets it the way he wants it."

More revealing was Davison's recollection of his visit to Sinatra's home at Coldwater Canyon. "It was night when the car drew up outside. It's a low, rakish building on top of a hill. We stepped into a massive lounge like a miniature ballroom. One wall is entirely of glass. We looked out on the lights of Hollywood and beyond the Pacific Ocean glistened in the moonlight. Just like fairyland. From the lounge window, steps lead down to a pale yellow, floodlit swimming pool. Beyond is Frank's private cinema. 'Now, how about a movie?' said Frank over the coffee and liqueur. He led the way to the cinema. We were shown a new picture starring Bette Davis and Joan Crawford called *Whatever Happened to Baby Jane?*"

Reporting on a dinner date with Sinatra at the famed Hollywood restaurant run by Sinatra's friends Mike and Gloria Romanoff, Davison said: "To walk in there with Frank was really something. Romanoff's is used to the famous but the attention and service he commands is really fantastic. Yet there is no 'side' with Frank. He's a multi-millionaire but he never throws his weight around. He's as casual as they come, but he can turn on the heat if the attention calls for it. But he's always the gentleman when ladies are around.

"His generosity is a byword. In fact, you have to be on your guard against admiring any gadget Frank may have in his house. He's quite likely to give it to you. And he won't take no for an answer."

Always fiercely protective of his rights to privacy, Sinatra belied his public image as a calculating tough guy; with his family he always commanded respect.

On 11 September 1960, daughter Nancy, then twenty, married singer Tommy Sands in Las Vegas. Frank gave his daughter away and Sammy Davis sang Frank's appropriate song for the occasion, "Nancy (With The Laughing Face)." In an interview with the US magazine *Redbook* later that year, Nancy declared that she, Tina and Frank Junior looked up to their father. "My mother [Nancy] and father refused to let their personal differences upset our lives. We're a family and we know it." Nancy added that there was more understanding between the five of them "than I've seen in many homes where there is no divorce."

Within three years, however, Frank Sinatra Junior was to be at the center of a tortuous experience that rocked the family and proved its solidarity. Frank Junior's career as a singer had been going for a year when, while appearing at Harrah's, Lake Tahoe, a knock at the door of his motel room announced: "Room Service." It was a hoodwink. Frank Junior had met his kidnappers. What followed showed the world a very different father: a frenzied father who sat jumping up and down when the phone rang incessantly as he awaited news of his son's safety. The ransom money he paid out was $240,000. Frank Sinatra Junior was freed, relatively unharmed. The birthday party of Frank Senior on 12 December at the Bel Air home of his ex-wife Nancy became a family celebration.

It was significant that the press, with whom Sinatra had a searing relationship, was highly supportive of Frank during this difficult period in the private life of a public figure. Journalists were conscious of doing what was possible to help ensure Frank Junior's safe return.

What was curious about Frank Sinatra, and what intimidated many, was his enviable ability to blend artistry and business. Unquestionably a giant of music and a prolific actor, he applied a ruthless eye to the statistics and strategy of his career.

That was particularly true of his record company. Reprise was a success and Sinatra believed firmly in delegation to his executives. Before long, the label's roster was formidable, adding Duke Ellington, Rosemary Clooney and ... Bing Crosby.

Intriguingly, Sinatra found time to record extensively during this frenetic period of his life, and he did so with inventiveness. A sentimental tribute album to the bandleader who had helped hoist him to the heights was called *I Remember Tommy.* With tasty arrangements by ex-Dorsey alumnus Sy Oliver, the revered arranger whose experience stretched back to the Jimmy Lunceford Orchestra in the 1930s, Sinatra recreated the moods, alternately languid or brassy and beefy, that he had enjoyed with the Dorsey band. Opening with the a cappella sound of "I'm Getting Sentimental Over You," Sinatra had a smile in his voice through "Without a Song," "I'll Be Seeing You," and the reflective, delightful "Polka Dots and Moondreams." The album ended as it began, with the Dorsey theme song. This was the heartfelt Sinatra, recording with style his debt to Dorsey, who had died on 26 November 1956.

A war had been raging with Frank's old label, Capitol, which pronounced his years with them *The Great Years* in a three-album set covering the period 1953 to 1960. But his Reprise productivity showed that he still had a tremendous amount to sing, and he came at it with gusto. While *No One Cares* and *Where Are You?,* his finest Capitol moments, would

be difficult to equal, he seemed under his own banner to be entering a phase that was more varied in style. Among his greatest albums, heading close to those Capitol classics, was an album called *Sinatra and Strings.* For this he employed Don Costa, an especially talented arranger who, Frank observed, injected special ingredients—not that Frank wanted to detract from any of the others, like Riddle or Jenkins, he added diplomatically. "But Don could write any sound I wanted in fifteen minutes: he knew exactly what I wanted."

Sinatra's association with Costa dated back to the early 1950s, when Frank's popularity was ebbing. Costa was a staff guitarist at a Boston radio station that Frank visited during a tour of towns and cities to promote himself with fifteen-minute programs.

"He had a full orchestra behind him and brought Axel Stordahl along with him," Costa said. "I was so impressed by Stordahl's orchestrations, by Sinatra's professionalism and the musicianly quality of the whole performance that I decided there and then to become an arranger."

In a whirlwind career, Costa moved to ABC Paramount and United Artists as director of artists and repertoire, working for such names as Eydie Gorme and Paul Anka. His début with the *Sinatra with Strings* album marked the start of a rich liaison. Costa always introduced the unexpected to his arrangements, which delighted Sinatra.

Costa stated that he loved working with Sinatra. "He was very good to me, made me very comfortable. I don't know really what else to say … except that he drinks Jack Daniel's whisky and has the initials JD on his blazer. I guess he must have part of the action."

Sinatra and Strings stands as an essential album, disproving instantly any theory that everything on Capitol was special and that he was "churning them out" on Reprise. The album notes summarize it: "You can't beat a parlay that ties greatness to greatness. For a song, what can top the best of Cole Porter, Harold Arlen, Jerome Kern, Richard Rodgers and Hoagy Carmichael? For interpretation, who but Sinatra? Together, the results are definitive.

"This is Sinatra dealing from the top of the deck, singing the songs that are 'beyond category' (which is Duke Ellington's eloquently descriptive term) … But there's something new here … for the first time Sinatra is backed by arrangements by Don Costa, who shows in this set that he is going to take his place in that very select group of great arrangers who have teamed so brilliantly with Sinatra in the past … Costa is no formula man. He varied his approach to suit the song." Sinatra led, but Costa wasn't far behind him in this mighty collection of monumental songs, from "I Hadn't Anyone Till You" and "Misty," through "Stardust" and a beautiful "Come Rain or Come Shine" on to "It Might as well be Spring" and a string-laden nod back to the James band standard, "All or Nothing at All."

There was also a concert tour with the legendary jazz bandleader Count Basie, with whom he also made a powerful album *Frank Sinatra and Count Basie.* This was a swinging affair, an underrated album at the time, featuring lively versions of "Please Be Kind," "Nice Work if You Can Get It" and "I Won't Dance." With creative arrangements by Neal Hefti, Sinatra seemed to achieve a new level of jazz-inflected energy.

It also had a song called "My Kind of Girl," with which British singer Matt Monro had a substantial hit. Described by many as a Sinatra soundalike, Monro made no secret of his near hero-worship of Sinatra. With the same timbre and using Sinatra's phrasing as his model, Monro had soared to the top of the best-sellers with "Portrait of My Love" in 1961.

Even the "Old Groaner" was signed to Reprise. Two trilbies in the studio set the tone for both style and substance.

In America, Frank was cast as the Chairman of the Board, but in Britain he was known by the more colloquial phrase, the Guv'nor, a phrase Matt Monro and many other singers and musicians used to describe him. That June of 1962, after the concerts, Sinatra plunged into his first recording session in London for what would become the album called *Great Songs from Great Britain.*

The atmosphere at the CTS studios in Bayswater was reverential, as if royalty were present. The arranger was Robert Farnon, a much-respected Canadian who lived in the Channel Islands and who had impressed Nelson Riddle enough to be commended to Frank. "He was thrilled with the wonderful scores," remembers Don Lusher, who played second trombone on the sessions. "I will always remember this as part of Frank Sinatra's courtesy: Harry Roche [first trombonist] had played that important solo in the middle of the song 'A Nightingale Sang in Berkeley Square.' And he was standing in the box, listening to his solo. Frank was obviously satisfied with what he [Roche] had done, but when the trombone solo ended, he pointed to Harry and asked: 'All right for you?'" Roche said yes; Frank said: "Print it," and the playback of the track was over, with musicians noting with pleasure that Sinatra still had time and respect for a musician.

The album was not vintage Sinatra. His voice had taken a pounding on the world tour, and it showed. The accolade for Britain was considerable, though, as he endorsed compositions by the country's songwriters on a selection that included "Roses of Picardy," "We'll Gather Lilacs," "The Very Thought of You" and "London by Night."

Robert Farnon commented on the experience: "Although Frank doesn't read music, he has one of the most fantastic musical minds I know. He'll pick up a tune in a flash, even if he hears it on the spot during rehearsals for the actual session."

Recalling that he first met Sinatra in New York when he was appearing with the Tommy Dorsey Orchestra, Farnon continued: "I remember he was singing 'I'll Never Smile Again.' He was a perfectionist then, and he still is. The only person he gets angry with on a session is himself. During our recordings, he ran into a little difficulty with the top notes and at one point, when we were all waiting breathlessly, he joked: 'Don't stare at the ceiling! Help me!' At the end of Frank's tour, he was very tired, I recall. He wasn't too happy about his voice on that occasion and the album wasn't released in the States. But it was in Europe."

Having flexed his muscle and proved he could run a winning record label, Sinatra surprised his public with remarks he made in July 1962.

"Eventually I want to be less and less before the public and more and more in the background," he told Joe Hyams for an article in the magazine *Cosmopolitan*. "I figure that as an actor and as a singer I have only a few more years to go. I'll be forty-seven in December. I won't really have had it, but you know, when I get around that age there's not much I'll want to play or could play." This was his first public indication of the possibility of retirement from singing that has punctuated the last thirty years.

"Frankly," he continued, "I'm fascinated with finances. I've been performing thirty years now and I'm getting a little lazy about this kind of work. I'd like to have something working for me for a change. But I'm narrowing the field of investments to show business. That interests me. I'm part of it. Anything else bores me and what bores me loses me."

Many artists, particularly those of his stature with an encyclopedic knowledge of his music, prefer to delegate their own business to others. Surrounded with good lieutenants though he was after leaving Dorsey to go solo, Sinatra always plunged into his deals with avid interest: from a TV show to a record date, from a season at Las Vegas to a movie, he knew precisely what he was worth and how much the deal was finally going to accrue.

Sentimental though he manifested himself in music, he took a hardheaded approach to business. Surprisingly, as it turned out, Reprise was not sacrosanct as his untouchable creation, for in mid-1963 rumors began to spread that he was selling the record company. It was merged with the mighty Warner Brothers, with Frank netting a multi-million dollar check for the sale, plus a continuing part ownership of the label. The Reprise logo remained but now it had the power of Warner behind it.

In Britain, the Beatles changed everything on the music landscape in 1963, sweeping in the new "beat group" bonanza, with records like "From Me to You," "Please Please Me" and "She Loves You." It would be another year before they hurtled across the Atlantic, reaching 73 million people via the Ed Sullivan television show and changing forever the world's perception of popular music.

Frank Sinatra was not alone in appearing to be in limbo while the revolution was happening. In the readers' poll conducted by the *Melody Maker* in Britain in 1963, he could finish only eighth in the male singer section. Ahead of him were Elvis Presley, Ray Charles, Cliff Richard, Roy Orbison, Bobby Vee, Buddy Holly and Del Shannon.

It was a watershed year in world events. The same year that he made a pivotal speech at the Berlin Wall, President Kennedy was assassinated in November. The Reverend Martin Luther King, Jr. made his "I have a dream" pronouncement on civil rights. A telephone "hot line" was established between the White House and the Kremlin.

Until that year, which gave us musicians both vocal and opinionated, artists were not expected to issue their opinions on anything beyond their work. Unexpectedly, just before the Beatles became the mouthpiece for the assertive young, Sinatra came forward to discuss things beyond his normal terrain. It happened in an interview with *Playboy* magazine in 1963. He spoke about religion: "I'm for anything that gets you through the night, be it

prayer, tranquillizers, or a bottle of Jack Daniel's. But to me religion is a deeply personal thing in which man and God go it alone together without the witch doctor in the middle. . . . I'm for decency—period." He supported everything that spread love and consideration for his fellow men. As a born Catholic, Frank declared that "when lip service to some mysterious deity permits bestiality on Wednesday and absolution on Sunday, cash me out."

He spoke about Communism, advocating that people should stop worrying about it and deal with the conditions that nurtured it; and he said of the Cold War between East and West that its continuation might be more effective as a peacekeeping method than "the dewy-eyed notion of total disarmament."

In a wide-ranging demonstration of self-analysis, Sinatra emerged as a highly principled man, well read, concerned about the world stage beyond his own. A year before the Beatles, and some years before Bob Dylan and other rock stars pontificated about the state of the earth in and out of their songs, Sinatra was, at age forty-eight, assertive and sassy.

Exploring his own work as a singer, he said he communicated the mood of the song by getting the audience involved, because he was himself involved. "Being an eighteen-carat manic depressive and having lived a life of violent emotional contradictions, I have an over-acute capacity for sadness as well as elation." What he sang, he stated emphatically, he believed. The fundamental difference between Sinatra's oeuvre and that of the Beatles and what followed lay in songwriting. Where Sinatra took the songs from the pens of geniuses like Gershwin and Porter, Cahn and Van Heusen, Rodgers and Hart, the 1960s generation wrote their own material.

The factor that separated Sinatra from hundreds of other fine singers, however, was that when he interpreted the compositions of others, he revealed much of himself. Clearly, he could sing only the kind of song that allowed him to penetrate his own soul.

Despite the thunder of the new music, Sinatra held his unassailable position in the mid-1960s as the world's heavyweight champion in solo singing. Winning the polls for him might have belonged to a different, pre-rock era, but his individuality meant he could not be toppled. In his movies, he played a happy bachelor in *Come Blow Your Horn* in 1963, as well as a cowboy in *Four for Texas,* in which his co-stars were Dean Martin, Anita Ekberg and Ursula Andress. The following year brought *Robin and the Seven Hoods.* With Dean Martin, Sammy Davis Junior and Peter ("Columbo") Falk, the film was a pastiche of Robin Hood set in Chicago. And in 1965, Sinatra portrayed an American Marine on a South Pacific island in *None but the Brave,* which he also produced; he was an Army colonel in *Von Ryan's Express,* which had him organizing an escape from an Italian prisoner-of-war camp. And he was a business tycoon in *Marriage on the Rocks,* which also featured Deborah Kerr and Dean Martin.

But always and forever, it is for his singing, his "vocalization" as he describes it, that history will reserve his place in the pantheon of entertainment. While his acting often entertained us, his singing moved us.

His talk in 1962 of "kicking himself upstairs" to consolidate his business activities at the expense of his active music-making continued to look hollow. In January 1966, *Disc Weekly,* a British music newspaper of which I was editor, published a special tribute to him, marking his fiftieth birthday and quarter century as an artist.

Pye Records, which distributed Reprise in the UK, launched a nationwide Sinatra Week, with the distribution of over 5,000 posters and 250,000 leaflets, the biggest promotion ever undertaken for a solo artist by the company. The release of what was then unique, a "double pack" anthology LP, plus an EP and singles, was joined by an NBC musical show, *Sinatra: A Man and His Music,* which was shown to record dealers, the press and disc jockeys. The album of the same name covered his career well; additionally there was a second album, called *My Kind of Broadway.* It was good, but less impressive than most of his work because the songs, like "Have You Met Miss Jones" and "Hello Dolly," hardly called for his personal clout. Launching the Sinatra event, Louis Benjamin, boss of Pye, remarked: "This is being done not only from a commercial aspect. Sinatra Week is being staged out of respect for him as an artist and also in appreciation of the way his company and now Warner Brothers work so closely with us."

If the tributes in *Disc Weekly* to Sinatra sounded idolatrous, it was because they came from keen students of his art. Matt Monro came clean about his unabashed love of the work of the singer whose style gave him direction: "Singers come and singers go," Monro wrote, "but as far as I'm concerned Frank Sinatra will always remain the epitome

Von Ryan's Express saw a hard-nosed performance from Sinatra, who played an American officer in a POW camp in Italy.

of vocal artistry. Why do I call him the Guv'nor? Because he has brought to pop songs a degree of integrity and professionalism that has elevated the idiom into an accepted art form.

"Ballads or swingers, and even novelty songs like 'Macdonald's Farm' take on new dimensions in his gifted hands and he has developed the uncanny knack of making you believe each song is directed personally at you. To me, Sinatra is the master and his international acclaim is a just reward for his unique talent."

Admitting that he was heavily influenced by Sinatra's work, Monro continued: "If you want to learn, you might just as well start at the top. Sinatra has wielded more influence on the song scene that any other singer alive."

Alan Dell, honorary president of the Sinatra Appreciation Society, weighed in with his tribute: "Many consider the period 1952 through to 1960 his greatest years. And yet today, at fifty, now the controller of his own record company, his interests diversified in real estate, an airline and film companies, he can glean the deepest meaning from a well-written lyric … and swing with the ring-a-ding-ding spontaneity of his individual assurance."

Several artists contributed to *Disc Weekly*'s salute. Bing Crosby said: "The most admirable thing about Frank is his great courage and determination. As a person he's a loyal and devoted friend, and an implacable enemy."

Doris Day described Frank as "a wonderful guy to work with. He has the biggest heart in the whole world. He'll do anything for you," while Judy Garland declared: "He's everything that's dear."

Mel Tormé, whose appearances Frank often attended, said: "He has that quality of singing in a packed theater and making every girl feel as if he's singing directly to her," while Harry James said of the ascent of his old band singer: "What's he been like through the years? He's always been the same. He didn't change one half an inch."

Sinatra's European representative Harold Davison spoke as one who had spent much time with him. "The essential factor about Frank Sinatra is his complete awareness about people and happenings on a very broad canvas. His extensive travels, his multi-varied business interests, his extreme range of acquaintances and friends have all brought something to his thinking and his conversation."

Well-read, he showed, said Davison, that his tentative association with journalism had left him with the facility to make a turn of phrase or color a story with personal observation: "He is humorous and has an edgy wit. Professionally he is always on time, if he has an appointment. But he is a man who knows what he wants. It is the directness, single-mindedness of Frank Sinatra which has caused him to attain commercial success, a complement to the artistic laurels he has gained."

In the entertainment business, Davison concluded: "There has never been one single person who has attained so much, achieved so much. He is respected by fellow artists and business associates as heartily and with as much fervour as he was accorded by the fans of the 1940s."

But it was the paper's record reviewer, Penny Valentine, who wrote the most pertinent words about a man twice her age. As *Disc Weekly*'s record reviewer, elsewhere she was considering the latest releases by such hip groovers as the Rolling Stones, the Supremes, Stevie Wonder, Little Richard, and the Lovin' Spoonful. Her appraisal of Sinatra's appeal to women was incisive.

Under the headline: "The Moment I Fell for Him!" Penny Valentine wrote that the moment his personality broke through to her, "he was being kicked and shoved around in a lot of nasty mud, during the rather vicious scene in *From Here to Eternity*. Before that, he was just someone my mother had gone potty about during the period in her life when she entered a jitterbug competition and won a butter dish. I never really fell for Sinatra the Voice. I still think that on the whole he's rather a dull singer, although one LP I'll always love is his *Only the Lonely*. Anything faster than Sinatra singing 'One for My Baby' must be written off … but on slow, sultry things that yearn, Sinatra has a quality of his own that, once I'd actually seen them on the screen, have a terrific fascination." Penny Valentine continued: "I am not blind. I have noted that Sinatra wears a toupee, that he has one slightly misshapen ear, that he is skinny and small. He is not handsome. And the attraction for Sinatra has nothing to do with his reputation as a raver, as a party giver, as a man who will be forever involved in controversy."

His appeal, she asserted, had nothing to do with the Sinatra legend. It was something more positive: "Ever since that first film part, I've understood the Ava Gardners of this world. Maybe it's the aggressive quality in that half-starved-looking figure that came from the not-so good part of New Jersey. Perhaps it's those clear, challenging eyes or the thin, hard mouth. Perhaps it's the obvious loneliness that lurks behind this man with a million friends."

Since his split from Ava, Sinatra was a bachelor about Hollywood and, seemingly, enjoying his independence. A workaholic, he found time to romance the South African dancer Juliet Prowse, whom he had met during the filming of *Can Can,* and observers said that they came close to marriage. There were dates, also, with singer-actress Dorothy Provine and actress Jill St. John. But the road to his third marriage was strewn with something Frank had become used to: controversy about his life off-stage.

He had first met Mia Farrow, an actress thirty years younger than him, at the studios of Twentieth Century-Fox in 1964. She was working on the hit television series *Peyton Place,* while Frank was acting nearby in the movie *Von Ryan's Express.* To the astonishment of his friends, and of columnists, their relationship proceeded to marriage. Mia, born on 9 February 1945, married Frank in California in 1966. But the marriage was to last a mere sixteen months. Mia was busy making movies, and in 1967 went to India to meditate alongside the Beatles, with the Maharishi Mahesh Yogi. By November 1967, they had separated. They were divorced in August 1968.

That year of 1966 was to be notable, also, for the expansion of the Sinatra name. Daughter Nancy, then aged twenty-five, sang "These Boots were Made for Walkin'" to the top of the charts; the catchy song sold more than 4 million copies world-wide. Written by producer Lee Hazelwood, it was Nancy's début.

Some thirty years Frank's junior, Mia Farrow became the new Mrs Sinatra in 1966. The marriage lasted a mere 16 months—what happened to the rhinestone-bejewelled outfit is anybody's guess.

When Nancy was cutting "These Boots Were Made for Walkin'," her father was recording at the same time in the studio next door.

"After I'd cut the track," Nancy said, "I went into my father's studio and over the intercom in the engineer's booth, I announced: 'I don't know what you're doing in here, Dad, but we're making hits next door.' Everybody thought it was very funny but it was the first time I felt really sure I had a chance for a hit. Actually funnier than that was that in my father's studio there were sixty musicians and a gallery full of spectators. In my studio I had a mike, an engineer and eight musicians."

"I was singing before I was talking," Nancy said in a newspaper interview. "My father gave me the whole thing: singing lessons, voice classes, piano lessons. I was just about in every choir there was. Was I brought up in a show-business family right from the word go? No, we were all given our own responsibilities at home. We were made to care for our home and wash the dishes after meals. Father didn't spoil us. We all went to ordinary public schools."

Nancy said that since she began a singing career her father "really hasn't interfered as much as people might think he would. He never tells me anything unless I really have a problem and go to him. The only time he might say anything is if I ever did anything horrible, in my personal life as well as my public. If I treated anyone badly he would step in straight away." People's reaction to her dad was strange, she continued: "The funniest thing about my father is the way people never expect him to be a human being. People are so taken with the image of Frank Sinatra that when they finally meet up with him and find out that he's flesh and blood and an absolutely marvellous man, they're stunned." Answering the taunts that she might have gained success because of her name, she was adamant: "It's not all that much of an advantage. People expect a lot from you when you've got a famous name. And they can be cruel when they find you're not that much better than all the rest." But she had never been tempted to change her name. "Why should I? I'm very, very proud of the Sinatra name."

Nancy's album following her hit became the fastest-selling album since the Beatles' *Rubber Soul.* Nancy's record topped the British chart in February 1966, edging ahead of Herb Alpert's "Spanish Flea" and Barbra Streisand's "Second Hand Rose." She was finally knocked from the top by the Rolling Stones with "19th Nervous Breakdown." Later that year, though, the Sinatra name was to return to the singles chart with astonishing power.

LOOK WHO'S BACK IN THE TOP TEN! screamed the front page headline in the *Melody Maker* on 21 May 1966. "SINATRA FOLLOWS DAUGHTER NANCY."

Sinatra had never achieved a number one position since the British charts began ten years earlier. "Strangers in the Night," a beguiling ballad that jumped in first at number thirty-four, then went to number ten, and in a feat equalled only by the Beatles, made the top on its third entry. In doing so, Sinatra ousted the Rolling Stones' "Paint It Black." Sinatra was comfortably ahead of such future evergreen singles as the Lovin' Spoonful's "Daydream," Bob Dylan's "Rainy Day Women," Cher's "Bang Bang," Simon and Garfunkel's "Homeward Bound" and the Mamas and Papas' "California Dreamin'." He had also leapfrogged his daughter's follow-up to "Boots," the too-similar "How Does That Grab You Darlin'." The label Reprise sat proudly atop the best-sellers, a pattern repeated around the world.

The music industry was absolutely agog at the unexpected return of fifty-year-old Sinatra to the limelight. In recent years, with the avalanche of American and British stars from Bobby Darin and the Beach Boys to the Supremes and the Four Tops, Sinatra had been considered an albums-only artist.

He had conquered with a haunting ballad that would become a popular standard. Although he did not write the song, Frank's twenty-eight-year-old producer, Jimmy Bowen, must be credited with discovering it and steering him towards it—and with moving speedily to ensure that he beat off heavy competition in a race to get "Strangers" to the top of the US chart; it hit the number one position on Billboard's Hot Hundred on 2 July 1966—eighteen weeks after Nancy's "Boots" had occupied that spot.

Left: Frank and Nancy performing on the TV special *A Man and His Music* in 1966.

Knowing that Bobby Darin and Jack Jones were also recording the song, Bowen called arranger Ernie Freeman and asked him to come up with an arrangement for Sinatra very quickly. Three days later, Bowen had a full orchestra in place by 5 p.m. and three hours later Sinatra arrived to record the song. He had finished his vocal track on tape by 9 p.m. and within twenty-four hours, radio stations across America were playing the Sinatra version.

And the lovelorn nature of the lyric was the kind of material Frank could have been singing at any stage of his career. It was a smash from the opening bars. The powerful, string-laden accompaniment underscored a rich performance … "strangers in the night, exchanging glances," he sang, in words that seemed to have been written especially for him.

The hit song was written by Bert Kaempfert, the German band leader who was also responsible for making the first recordings by the Beatles when they were in Hamburg long before they scored a big success. Bowen, the husband of another Reprise artist, the respected singer Keely Smith, originally heard the song as only a melody, played for him by Kaempfert's American publisher. The music was planned for a movie that Kaempfert was scoring in Hollywood, called *A Man Could Get Killed*.

Sinatra singing with Frank Junior, proving that it wasn't only daughter Nancy who inherited the musical talent.

When he heard the instrumental theme, Bowen recalls, "I was busted over it and said to Hal Fein, head of Roosevelt Music, the publishers for Kaempfert: 'I want this for Sinatra.' A month later lyrics were written: I showed it to Frank and he flipped over it as well, so we got together with Ernie Freeman, our arranger, and we cut the song on April 11.

"Frank loved it the first time he heard it," Bowen continued. "I don't know if he thought it would be this big, but when he and I went over the arrangement we discussed the kind of thing that could *make* it big. We did it more commercial than the Bert Kaempfert version. We accented the fourth beat. Bert did it with a definite two-four feel. Frank's record has a kind of syncopated feeling but it actually isn't that. It's just a heavy accent on the fourth. It's the way I felt the song. It makes a flow. If you use a two-four beat, it chops the song up. If you notice the way we did the strings, there's a continuous musical background throughout the song. The melody never stops. It's either the cellos, the violas or the violins."

Twelve violins, four violas and four cellos were used. "We used some at all times behind Frank," Bowen recalled. "It gives a nice kind of floating effect. We also used four French horns, four guitars, bass, drums, piano and two percussion."

In the hothouse of popular music and rock 'n' roll that characterized the mid-l960s, "Strangers in the Night" met an often cynical response among other artists. Dusty Springfield said: "I don't like the record. In the first place, I don't rate it as a good song. It doesn't hit me at all and I don't think it bears repeated listening." Ray Davies of the Kinks remarked: "It's not a top-quality type record, not one of Sinatra's best." And Alan Price, at that time keyboard player with the Animals, predicted wryly: "It may do something on the strength of his daughter's publicity. It'll make the Light Programme's late night shows, things like that." There was more than a degree of petulance among rock 'n' rollers who saw a man of fifty sweeping to the top with a haunting ballad. For the next thirty years, they would have to tolerate the fact that "Strangers in the Night" by Frank Sinatra would indeed be continually played around the world as an all-time classic. In the mid-l960s, as in the early 1940s, Sinatra was showing that when he sang a beautifully crafted love song, he transcended the whims of fashion.

For songwriters, having Sinatra's name on a song has been an accolade. Don Black, the British lyricist who collaborated with Andrew Lloyd Webber on *Sunset Boulevard,* has also worked with Henry Mancini, Jule Styne, Quincy Jones and Barbra Streisand. Sinatra's interpretation of Black's classic film theme "Born Free" was a mixed blessing to the writer. "He's the greatest storyteller, a lyric writer's dream," Black says, "but I was very disappointed when he recorded 'Born Free.' He did it as an up-tempo version. It's not the most romantic song, it's more of an heroic song; but you don't need Sinatra's signature on it."

But Sinatra, always the iconoclastic warrior, set his own agenda. Sometimes his acerbic remarks would wound, and Don Black recalls a recording session in California in the late 1960s. "Jimmy Bowen was the producer; he was married to Keely Smith at the time, and at this session there was an audience of élite personalities. Sinatra liked to sing to an audience. I remember Yul Brynner hanging around Sinatra in a sycophantic way, taking photos of everybody. I sat down with Jack McGraw, who had taken me along. He used to work for Sinatra's Reprise label in Los Angeles. And Sinatra walked in and started singing a dreadful song; it was at the time he was singing real rubbish."

Despite that, the basic pleasure of Black's experience at witnessing Sinatra in action was spoiled when the singer said to producer Bowen through the control-room glass, and within earshot of everyone present: "Where did you get this drummer? From the Yellow Pages?"

There was, Black recalls, "the most terrible feeling of 'My God!' I thought: what a cruel guy. Everyone laughed, because you had to do that, but I remember thinking of the old saying: Never shake hands with your heroes because some of the guilt might rub off. From then on, I never wanted to meet anyone famous."

After the session, however, Sinatra redeemed himself in the view of Don Black. Adjourning to Martoni's off Sunset Boulevard, a favorite restaurant of Sinatra, the British writer was introduced to him properly. "He was delightful, lovely, funny, with a string of one-liners, sipping Jack Daniel's. He was just like the image you had of him from all those movies. That took the sting out of the earlier encounter."

Sinatra held court at the restaurant: rather like the King and his courtiers. People went to his table. "He was in charge of the place," Black muses. "Everyone within twenty blocks knew Sinatra was in Martoni's."

Sinatra

The Voice

What we see and hear is the man as the artist. His first incarnation had been as "The Vulnerable Tough." In the 1960s he matured as "The Swinger" and "The Chairman of the Board." While the movies poured out as well as the music, his private life, too, was played out in public, beginning his fractious relationship with the media. Establishing his own record label, winning movie awards, singing his way to the top on "Strangers in the Night," he rode out the new rock 'n' roll revolution. And then he announced his retirement. But it was not to be. His appetite for the stage was insatiable right into the 1990s, and Sinatra's reign as the most popular solo singer in his field remains secure.

1956-95

1956

"You're sensational." In *High Society* Sinatra delivered a superb Cole Porter score, alongside Grace Kelly, who later became Princess Grace of Monaco, and supported him in his charitable works.

Sinatra's sartorial
sharpness was
characterized by
his carefully tilted
trilby and the
immaculate suits.

The bittersweet pleasures of fame and fortune intensely impacted Sinatra in the Sixties. On 8 December 1963—just shortly after the Kennedy assassination—Frank Junior was kidnapped at a Lake Tahoe resort. Working with FBI officers, Sinatra personally handed over the $240,000 ransom, Frank Junior was released, and the kidnappers were soon apprehended. Below: the Dual Ghia was one happy indulgence amongst several spectacular automobiles owned by Sinatra.

"Most of our best numbers were in what I call the tempo of the heart beat. That's the tempo that strikes people easiest because, without their knowing it, they are moving to that pace all their working hours. Music to me is sex—it's all tied up somehow and the rhythm of sex is the heart beat, I always have some woman in mind for each song I arrange; it could be a reminiscence of some past romantic experience or just a dream scene I build in my imagination.

"Frank undoubtedly brought out my best work. He is stimulating to work with. You have to be right on mettle all the time. The man himself somehow draws everything out of you.... he'd never record before 8.00 p.m. and we'd knock off sometimes after 11.00. We'd get about four numbers finished at a session with an average of three takes a number." Nelson Riddle

1967

In his later movies Sinatra played a variety of detectives. *Tony Rome* was the first of these. Set in Miami—above, on set with Jill St John—the film recalled a Chandler-like landscape taken from earlier *films noir.*

As Bing Crosby had predicted, just two years after Frank's supposed retirement in 1973, "Ol' blue eyes was back," the voice more mellow but firmly authoritative.

In an emotional
"farewell" concert
at the Los Angeles
Music Center, on
13 June, he gave a
vintage performance.

In 1985 President Ronald Reagan presented the Presidential Medal of Freedom—the Nation's highest civilian award—to Frank Sinatra at The White House. "I have known Frank Sinatra for a number of years," the President said. "I am aware of the incidents, highly publicized quarrels with photographers, nightclub scrapes, etc., and I admit it is not a lifestyle I emulate or approve. However, there is a less publicized side to Mr Sinatra which justice must recognize. I know of no one who has done more in the field of charity than Frank Sinatra."

"For over three
decades I have had
the great and good
fortune to enjoy a
rich, rewarding and
deeply satisfying
career."

That's Life

"How Old Am I?"—a poignant Gordon Jenkins song—was sung on an introspective album called September of My Years. *The title track would become a favorite among the Sinatra cognoscenti. This collection of unexpected songs found the fifty-year-old maestro more self-analytical than ever.*

Included was a particularly soul-searching ballad into which Frank invested palpable feeling. "It Was a Very Good Year," he sang. Curiously, he was looking inwards at a time when his position as a classy, unclassifiable singer seemed more tenable than ever. Whether he had been serious, three years earlier, about his desire to pull away from music making in favor of becoming a businessman, he was yanked into action by a simple factor: public demand.

A toast to all the superb songwriters and composers, as always acknowledged by Sinatra in appreciation of each song he has performed. The reigning monarchs of jazz, at right—Sinatra, Fitzgerald and Basie, sold out at Caesar's Palace, Las Vegas, in 1974.

In 1965 he appeared at the Newport Jazz Festival. The heady allure of being loved equally by musicians and the community of show business, plus the public, proved irresistible.

A remarkably successful appearance with the Count Basie Band, with whom he also toured, demonstrated to the jazz festival purists that, popular singer though he was, he had a claim on the jazz fraternity too. Always improvisational, Sinatra could fairly be said to be close enough to jazz to justify his place at the festival, despite the hoots of derision that came with the announcement of his appearance.

If Count Basie, with whom he made a splendidly jazzy album, did not find Sinatra's company incompatible, then Frank was a jazzman by association. And anyone who had sat, as Frank had, spellbound at the voice of Billie Holiday in the clubs of New York's 52nd Street, and worked with the bands of Dorsey and James and Goodman, surely had more than a foot in the jazz camp.

Part of the jazz ethos in those years was that if music was popular, it could not be called jazz. Ella Fitzgerald, Mel Torme and Peggy Lee exploded that myth, and Louis Armstrong famously made commercial records like "Hello Dolly" and "It's a Wonderful World" that imposed his jazz style on popular song.

Unacceptable to the purists, perhaps, was that Sinatra was a multi-millionaire success. To many, jazz implied a minority music. But as jazz pianist Nat King Cole and jazz guitarist George Benson showed, achieving popularity did not necessarily mean forfeiture of any jazz credentials. It wasn't so much what they said as the way they said it: they became popular singers with a jazz base.

Sinatra always held those same cards, too: if jazz and the blues stemmed from giving music a personal imprint, which was replete with feeling, then Sinatra was much more than a mere "pop singer."

He continued to keep company with jazz people in the mid-1960s, touring with a drummer who had been with him in the Dorsey band, Buddy Rich, and his group. Since Sinatra was on record as saying that great jazz was dead, it mattered not a jot whether he was classified among the élite of that genre. What was disappointing was the mean spirit of the self-appointed jazz committees who turned up their noses at Sinatra. His enormous impact on the crowd at Newport was sweet music to an artist who, like his friend Duke Ellington, believed there were only two types of music: good and bad.

**Working with
Count Basie in
1965 reaffirmed
Sinatra's affinity
with jazz people.**

Sinatra's progeny continued to move closer to his turf. In 1965, twenty-one-year-old Frank Sinatra Junior made his début with an album (on Reprise) called *Young Love for Sale.* "He calls himself a diligent apprentice," the album announced. For more than two years, young Frank had been on the road, travelling 274,000 miles to twenty-one different countries and to forty American states.

Frank Junior's first record was a creditable selection of up-tempo and warm ballads, from "Love for Sale" to "I Only Have Eyes for You," from "In the Still of the Night" to "Falling in Love with Love." Like his father, Junior wanted to tough it out as a band singer, so he bravely joined the band of tenor saxophonist Sam Donahue, who had long experience alongside such venerable figures as Gene Krupa and Woody Herman.

Music had always been in Frank Junior's bones. Throughout school, he had always been using his voice. When he was about seventeen he "decided to investigate whether I had any talent at all." Noting that almost every big singer grew up singing in a band, he explained: "That's why I joined Sam Donahue's band. It might be twenty years too late but the experience of singing with a band can't do me any harm."

The album presented us with a time warp, with a young man singing with band accompaniment, uncannily like a singer with the Dorsey band. As time passed, Frank Junior would emerge as a singer with individuality, albeit within the same creative framework as his father.

Through the years, it has been astonishing to watch Sinatra cut a swathe through all the trends, musical and cultural, to demonstrate the commercial power of straight popular music. Even in 1967, when psychedelia entered the dictionary as a force in stream-of-consciousness rock music, Sinatra broke through with another million-seller.

This time, it was a novelty sound, a duet with daughter Nancy. "Somethin' Stupid," a simple ballad with attractive instrumental arrangement by Billy Strange and cute production by Jimmy Bowen, Frank's producer, and Lee Hazelwood, Nancy's producer, took father and daughter to the top of the best-sellers in America in April 1967, securing a Gold Record for them. With thirteen weeks in the US charts and five weeks at the top, it racked up a quarter of a million sales in Britain, where it also went to the top of the charts.

The record was made in a mere thirty-five minutes, perhaps setting another kind of record for the speediest disc hit ever. Nancy pointed out with some pride that her Dad had not helped her get started on record—"Boots" was done solo by her—but that he had waited until she had made an impact alone before stepping into a studio with her.

A good father and friend to both daughters, Tina and Nancy, Frank recorded "Somethin' Stupid," in duet with Nancy, and it topped the charts around the world. Nancy, shown earlier at high school, right, was introduced to the art of broadcasting with her father and pursued her own solo singing career.

"My Way" crept up on Frank Sinatra as his autobiographical anthem. He did not plan it that way, but the words, the texture, the timing of the song had an inevitability for him that seemed perfect at the end of his turbulent 1960s.

Rarely could a song have been tailored so perfectly for one man's quest. In a private and public life that had undergone the fiercest scrutiny, and from which he had emerged above all as an artist who had

already transcended his time, Sinatra stood alone, incomparable, indefatigable.

And now, he sang, the end was near, and so he faced the final curtain. . . . "My Way" had been written in 1967 as a French song, called "Comme d'Habitude," by Claude François and Jacques Revaux, with words by the French lyricist Gilles Thibaut. Two years later, the Canadian singer Paul Anka, famous for his hit record "Diana," added the English words that sounded as if they had been honed to perfection as Frank Sinatra's musical epitaph. Paul Anka took the song to Frank when he was appearing in Las Vegas. Frank liked it enough to record it within forty-eight hours—but he never expected it to explode over the radio so fast or to become so closely identified with him.

He'd lived a life that was full, he'd travelled each and every highway … and he'd done it his way.

Sinatra has said that he certainly did not adopt the song as an autobiographical finale. But that's how the world construed it as the years passed. "It was not written for me . . . . any remarks in it are not my own, they are from the lyricist," Sinatra has said. The sparkling arrangement was by Don Costa.

At the time of its release in the summer of 1969, sandwiched between such records as the Beatles' chart-topping "Get Back" and Simon and Garfunkel's "The Boxer," Sinatra's single went virtually unnoticed by the critics. But the public reacted positively: it rose to number four in the British charts and peaked at number twenty-seven in America. In Britain it had sold a million by 1970 and was the country's top sheet music seller in 1969. By 1971 it had racked up more formidable statistics, holding the record at the time for the longest stay of any song in the British charts (122 weeks into 1971), by which time there were at least 100 other versions. It was a natural choice of hundreds of ballad singers in concert and cabaret, yet it would remain, forever, irrevocably Frank Sinatra's.

"My Way" could have been a stunning valediction. How odd it is to reflect that, a full twenty-five years after that song appeared to be saying goodbye, Sinatra would be active with the *Duets* albums, appearing in concerts, and as fashionable among people in their mid-twenties as when he first peeked out from the curtains at the Paramount in New York five decades earlier.

As "My Way" climbed the charts, a wave of interest in his concerts began again in London. His friend Harold Davison flew to the US to plan for Frank's return to Britain for his first concerts since 1962. There was great anticipation among admirers. Sinatra Music Society president Alan Dell stated at that time: "A whole generation of kids are going to have the chance of experiencing the Sinatra magnetism for the first time. And I don't think it will be the last time. Sinatra said on his fiftieth birthday that he would go on as long as he can and he's certainly proving it. People who have not seen Sinatra should not miss this chance. The man is magnetic on stage. He moves with the minimum of gestures yet his presence is simply spellbinding."

Britain's wait of eight years for the return of the singer ended on 7 May with two nights of concerts at the same Royal Festival Hall, London, that had thrilled Frank with its exceptional acoustics back in 1962. Attended by Princess Margaret, the show I saw was in aid of the National Society for the Prevention of Cruelty to Children, a continuation of the theme of Sinatra's world tour to benefit children in 1962.

The Festival Hall seats 3,000. Manifestly it was too small to accommodate the number of applicants for tickets and Harold Davison declared: "I could have filled Wembley Stadium twice over." Tickets were selling on the black market at ten times their face value.

Heralding his arrival, Laurie Henshaw, in a *Melody Maker* tribute called "The Magic of Sinatra," wrote: "More than as a singer, Sinatra communicates as a personality; this is one of the qualities that women, particularly, are quick to detect. There's a touch of 'devil' in him that's calculated to make even the most devoted housewife want to pack her bags. One feels that many of them would hardly trouble to leave a note on the bedside table. As one put it to me: 'Maybe Frank isn't the best-looking man in the world. I don't even care whether or not he wears a toupee. He just has to open his mouth.'"

Extending the admiration to his musicianship, Henshaw cited just a few colleagues of Sinatra, Sy Oliver, Count Basie, Alec Wilder and Nelson Riddle, and concluded: "No one is quicker to spot a phoney than a musician. There could be no greater testimony to Sinatra's towering talent than that it should receive such universal acclaim from those who know . . . . Dismiss, if you wish, those matrons with the blue-rinse hairdos and pink stoles who were prepared to write blank cheques for Sinatra tickets. But it's impossible to ignore the accolades that have been heaped upon Sinatra from those professional contemporaries in the music business who really know where it's at."

The perfection of a Sinatra concert never came accidentally. Rather, his performances have always been the result of forensic attention to detail. In London, there would be four rehearsals, two first without the singer, then two with him. The orchestra, consisting of fifty-five musicians plus his regular musical director Bill Miller (piano) and Irving Cottler (drums), were joined by top pedigree British musicians of the caliber of trumpeters Kenny Baker and Stan Roderick and trombonist Harry Roche

Combined with the majesty and tension of the event, the example set by Sinatra's regular musicians would have intimidated lesser players than the British contingent. "They were always first on the stand, tootling away before the rehearsal, a shining example of musicianship and professionalism," recalls Don Lusher, the veteran trombonist, formerly of the Ted Heath Orchestra. After dozens of concerts in Sinatra's band, travelling around Europe in a twenty-year period, Lusher reflects passionately on his years playing alongside the singer.

"The conductor would tell us what Frank liked and didn't want, and it was such a good band rehearsals would often finish early because everyone got it right. Playing the music by those arrangers like Nelson Riddle, Gordon Jenkins, Axel Stordahl, Don Costa … players like Bobby Lambe [trombonist] and I were pretty well schooled, but sometimes we'd not be playing and look at each other with tears of joy rolling down our cheeks. The arrangements were that good."

Instructions to the musicians were precise. "He likes that part this way; whatever you do don't play loudly here." Sinatra's assistants left nothing to chance, monitoring the nuances of every section of the orchestra.

"And then, you'd come along for afternoon rehearsal and see someone sitting beside you, dressed casually but expensively. It was Sinatra," smiles Don Lusher. "He'd start singing along with the band. And though this is to say nothing against those wonderful conductors, who had everything down to a tee, Sinatra would very soon pull lots of things apart. He would conduct himself, and say what he wanted, mostly to exaggerate the dynamics. He seems to have no time at all for wall-to-wall music. When it's soft it's ultra-soft. When it's loud, it's almost full-out. When it's out of tempo, as in a verse, you've got to play as if you, the musician, were HIM: you must be absolutely together. He plays with the phrasing. Pushing a little here and there, telling a story." As in his personality, definition, light and shading, texture and uncompromising positivism marked out Sinatra's stance on stage.

"It had to be not just right, but *dead right,*" Don Lusher says. "He would spend a great amount of time establishing that. If the rehearsal went well, Sinatra would nod his head. If it was the slightest bit out, he would yell. He's a perfectionist. He would certainly point out if *anything* was wrong, from the dressing room to the lights, the sound."

Though he "was not the life and soul of the party," Sinatra would sometimes dabble in light conversation with the musicians. "In some rehearsals, I'd be playing away, concentrating, sitting at the end of a row of players. And I'd come to the end of a solo and sitting there beside me was Sinatra. 'Good morning,' he'd say, and that would be that."

Even for a musician like Lusher, the moment of realization that this was a major event came after he had done a trombone solo. "I remember the first time I played the famous trombone solo in 'I Got You Under My Skin.' He usually looks at the soloist: I was looking at him and caught those Sinatra eyes. And they went right through me. I looked away," says Lusher, laughing at the memory. "I never, ever looked at him again when I was playing anything. I daren't!"

Reviewing the midnight show at the Royal Festival Hall in the *Melody Maker* as "a masterly performance by a show business phenomenon," I wrote that Sinatra was not a god to be exalted. "But musically, he stands completely apart from the swingeing publicity that has bedevilled his credibility all these years. The man has a magic, and it does not need qualifying with any reference to his fifty-four years. He's not just 'good for his age.' He's good.

"After a pleasing first half from the Count Basie Band, Sinatra strode on stage after the interval. A small, lone yet commanding figure, he bounced into 'I've Got the World on a String' and did not speak to the audience until seven songs later and then only to introduce 'Autumn Leaves' by saying: 'This is a lovely song.' His voice, at first coarse and

Sinatra, the hip hippie, at his London concerts in Nehru shirt and bejewelled like a czar. By this time he had the world on a string.

sounding tired, seemed to improve as the songs passed: 'I Get a Kick out of You,' 'At Long Last Love,' 'Don't Worry 'Bout Me,' 'Fly Me to the Moon' [this with beautifully rich string accompaniment], 'Street of Dreams' [at an awkward tempo] … 'Pennies from Heaven' and 'My Kind of Town.'

"Then came a dull middle period, featuring 'Yesterday,' 'This Is All I Ask' and a boring 'Try a Little Tenderness' for which guitarist Al Viola came to the front. Maybe the songs had been chosen to contrast with the swinging material earlier, but the programming was wrong because the pace slackened.

"But he was soon back with winners like 'Moonlight in Vermont,' 'You Make Me Feel So Young,' 'You've Got Me Under Your Skin,' 'Please be Kind' and 'The Lady Is a Tramp.' And when he came back to a rapturous encore with 'My Way,' the volume of applause was proof that he had been something of a hit."

I could not but wonder if the crowd had been wallowing in nostalgia, nodding with romantic flashbacks to those parties in the late 1950s and pre-Beatles 1960s, when the album *Songs for Swingin' Lovers* was *de rigueur.* Partly. But he vanquished all such qualifications by his genius. "He obviously listens closely to all the musicians in the band," I noted from the concert, "and his timing is personal and near-perfect. Even those who don't particularly care for his voice must admit that his phrasing is totally self-styled and original; and he relaxes behind that beat with the confidence and assurance of a man who lives dangerously but always gets back in time."

The factors that made Sinatra a living legend were, I added, difficult to pinpoint because it was hard to describe an aura. If that was true in 1970, it is even more valid now.

While he has been considered a formidable adversary, Sinatra has amassed an army of people who testify to his generosity. In and out of show business, his friends have outvoted his foes. From Judy Garland and her daughter Liza Minnelli, from obscure musicians whom he has supported in times of foul weather, through to political figures from Kennedy to Reagan, Sinatra is an active ally. The number of people who testify to the man's largesse, and his resolution to "be there" for those whom he values in their neediest moments, would fill a chapter.

Two male singers had particular cause to respect him for something beyond his art. Both masters of their territory, America's Tony Bennett and Britain's Matt Monro had stories to tell of Sinatra's huge impact on them.

In an interview with the magazine *Life* in 1965, Frank Sinatra stated unequivocally that Tony Bennett was the best singer in the business. Sinatra added that Bennett's vocal work excited him more than that of anyone else. For Bennett, eleven years Sinatra's junior, it was a bewildering if magnificent accolade. In 1962, he had enjoyed a great breakthrough with his signature song, "I Left My Heart in San Francisco," but, with the onslaught of the Beatles era, his style of ballad-singing had been rather obscured. Bennett's sons loved the Beatles but Tony had grown up on Sinatra: he had even seen him and spoken to him back at the Paramount Theatre in New York when Sinatra was with the Dorsey band. Bennett had always heeded his crucial advice to him at that time. Sinatra told him not to worry about being nervous because such a natural characteristic showed the public that the artist cared. Sinatra added, importantly, that it was when the artist was clearly *not* nervous that the public grew suspicious.

Another piece of Sinatra advice stuck with Bennett: never compromise with your choice of material. Choose only the best songs.

Sinatra's valuable endorsement of Bennett reshaped the singer's motivation. Already respected as a warm-voiced individualist, Bennett improved because of the growth of his self-esteem. On his concerts, Sinatra reiterated his praise, and later he would point Bennett towards a particular song which Sinatra had sung but which sounded as if it had been constructed uniquely for the Bennett timbre and delivery. This was the Michel Legrand composition, with lyrics by Marilyn and Alan Bergman, called "How Do You Keep the Music Playing." Sinatra did justice to the gorgeous, philosophical song. But when Tony Bennett did it, it took on a richer perspective.

Returning Sinatra's tribute in his own way, Bennett recorded an album in 1992 called *Perfectly Frank.* Featuring the "torch and saloon songs of Sinatra," this twenty-four-track selection ranged from Frank's earliest work, such as "East of the Sun" and "Nancy" through to "Here's That Rainy Day" and "One for My Baby." The choice of songs was carefully made, avoiding the instantly identifiable Sinatra classics like "Come Fly with Me" and "Witchcraft," Bennett heading instead for the more intense works of Sinatra.

In his self-written notes accompanying the tribute, Bennett recalled the night of 13 October 1974, when he was sitting watching television with his mother. Tragically bedridden, she had her entire family around her. "Her only entertainment was watching television, so we were anxiously tuned in to a music special called *The Main Event.* The performer was Sinatra,

the Champ, at Madison Square Garden. We were so enthralled with his performance. Suddenly, in between two marvellous songs, he belts out that I'm his favorite singer. Taken by surprise, I looked over at my Mom. Her eyes opened almost as big as her heart. It was one of the great moments of my life. I'll never forget what he did for me that day."

Writing of the "warm side to Sinatra that has never been played up properly," Bennett continued: "Being on the inside of show business, I can't begin to tell you how many human stories I've heard about the silent Sinatra. Highly philanthropic, he downplays the thousands of worthwhile benefits he has done over the years. As a private man with a profound sense of loyalty to his friends, he never touts the generosity he has shown to those he loves. That's the man."

Matt Monro, the best British singer in the field, idolized Sinatra. He had a similar timbre, enunciated his lyrics with the élan that the master had handed down, and demonstrated excellent taste in his material, scoring hits in the early 1960s with "Portrait of My Love," "Softly as I Leave You" and "My Kind of Girl."

The die had been cast for Monro as a Sinatra clone from the start of his career. "Indirectly, it was through Sinatra that I gained one of my first major breaks in Britain," Matt Monro told me. "I was requested to sing briefly on the Peter Sellers album, *Songs for Swinging Sellers,* and was asked to deliberately, 'do a Sinatra.' On the label credits I appeared under the name of Fred Flange.

Arriving on location
for *Lady in Cement*
with his stand-in
(front) and protective
escorts.

"Well, the record was released and everybody thought it really was Sinatra on the disc. Finally it came out in the press that I was the singer and my stock really soared."

In February 1966 Matt signed a $200,000 deal with Capitol, Sinatra's label. It was a two-pronged triumph for Matt: he was joining his favorite singer's stable; and Capitol envisioned him as a natural successor to Nat King Cole, who died in 1965. Matt's début single was his manager Don Black's composition "Born Free." "Matt made some albums in the States with Sinatra's sidekicks, such as Billy May and the producer Dave Cavanaugh," Don Black says. "It was all going great for Matt but unfortunately Matt never quite grasped the potential he had. Though Matt had been talking about Sinatra all his life, he had never met him. As his manager, I wanted to arrange it but never, ever could. When Sinatra was in London, I arranged for Matt to have tickets, but somehow we never went backstage afterwards." Twice on an American tour, Matt missed Frank by a matter of minutes. Monro recalled: "The first occasion was when my wife Mickie and I were holidaying in Palm Springs in November 1963. We decided to go to do a nightclub and narrowed our choice of venue to two. We went along to one, only to learn the next morning that Sinatra had been appearing at the other.

"Then a friend kindly fixed for me to visit Frank on the set of a film he was making in Hollywood. But shooting on the movie finished a few days earlier than expected … and as I flew into Los Angeles, Sinatra flew out. Some day, I hope, I'll get around to meeting the Guv'nor. I've been in this business for some time and am expected to be a bit blasé about meeting stars. But believe me, when we do meet, I'll be the happiest man in town."

Sadly, that never happened. But when Matt Monro was dying in London's Cromwell Hospital in 1985 at the appalling premature age of forty-eight, and facing his illness with tremendous spirit, Don Black felt it would be good to get a message from Sinatra to him. Black wrote to Sinatra's manager and a cable followed: HANG IN THERE. YOU'RE THE GREATEST, said the message from Sinatra, who signed himself: FRANK, THE YOUNG BOY SINGER. "Matt was so touched," remembers Don Black.

"Put Your Dreams Away (For Another Day)," sang Frank Sinatra, so many times. The song, which he had recorded in 1957, was redolent of its quaint era, when moon and June and tenderness were part of popular song. Sinatra always interpreted it with a curious feeling of special attachment to the song's sentiment. It would always remain special to him. "Dear

old theme song," he says when introducing it. "We've come a long way together, you and I. All the way from nowhere to somewhere. And you stuck by me every inch of the way. You're a little beat-up now, a little wrinkled and grey. But I love you, old buddy, I love you. . . ."

In March 1971, when he announced his retirement, the title of the song seemed to take on a new meaning. He was fifty-five. Frank's father had died from a heart attack on 24 January 1969. Could that have triggered his decision to call it a day?

To Sinatra followers, news of his retirement had its merits. The man who had always stood for immaculate taste in music had released two inferior albums in 1970. First a nondescript collection called *Watertown,* a concept album about a broken marriage in a small town: it did not have one memorable song. And then, with *Sinatra and Company,* he seemed to have been sucked into presenting himself as far too contemporarily hungry.

The tenor of both albums simply did not sit well with an artist who had spent three decades interpreting the majestic lyrics and melodies of irreplaceable composers like Rodgers and Hart and Cahn and Van Heusen. On *Sinatra and Company,* which pairs Frank with bossa nova supremo Antonio Carlos Jobim, with arrangements by Eumir Deodato, the attempt to relax Frank into bossa rhythms led to soporific versions of songs that, lacking light and shade, did not suit Sinatra's style. Five of the songs in this style were threadbare, redeemed only by "Wave" and "One Note Samba."

Even with Don Costa's sparky production and arrangement on the other side, Sinatra sounded uninspired by the songs and consequently lackluster and sterile. Two songs

Frank's father Martin had followed his career with care. His death in 1969 perhaps signalled Frank's own mortality and led to his proposed retirement from the stage.

by Paul Ryan, son of Marion Ryan, did not fit Sinatra: the corny "I Will Drink the Wine" and the weak "Sunrise in the Morning" were simply unconvincing and below Frank's standard. He played around with John Denver's "Leaving on a Jet Plane." Only a moving tribute to Billie Holiday called "Lady Day," written by Bob Gaudio and Jake Holmes, made the album worth buying.

Against this disappointing turn of events on the recording front, Sinatra's retirement was not unwelcome to students of his career. It was a period of profound change in the music world: the Beatles had split acrimoniously the previous April. Elton John and Rod Stewart were emerging to dominate the male rock star field for the next twenty-five years and beyond. Other music that would endure was taking root: soft rock from the Eagles, inventive work from guitarist Eric Clapton, the timeless popular records of the Carpenters (whose number one hit "Close to You" was recorded by Sinatra). Tom Jones, whose verve Sinatra admired, had carved a strong career since the 1960s, and stalwarts such as Vic Damone and Jack Jones remained popular in the ballad field. But, overall, the music scene was beating to a different drum in the early 1970s and it seemed timely for Sinatra to say farewell with dignity. He did so with aplomb, in a public statement beamed around the world's media: "I wish to announce, effective immediately, my retirement from the entertainment world and public life.

"For over three decades I have had the great and good fortune to enjoy a rich, rewarding and deeply satisfying career as an entertainer and public figure. It has been a fruitful, busy, uptight, loose, sometimes boisterous, occasionally sad, but always exciting three decades. There has been, at the same time, little room or opportunity for reflection, reading, self-examination and that need which every thinking man has for a fallow period, a long pause in which to seek a better understanding of changes occurring in the world.

"This seems a proper time to take that breather and I am fortunate enough to be able to do so. I look forward to enjoying more time with my family and dear friends, to writing a bit—perhaps even to teaching." He thanked his many admirers. And that was that; or so it seemed. Observers pointed out that, aside from his obvious reasons for retiring, Frank had had an operation on his right hand in the previous June, for Dupytren's contracture, a complaint that caused the fingers and muscles to contract.

Frontpaging the news, the magazine *Perfectly Frank,* organ of the newly named Sinatra Music Society based in Britain (honorary president: Sinatra), intoned somberly: "The final chapters in a voluminous book about the highly memorable, action-packed,

Opposite: The end of the road? "I look forward to enjoying more time with my family and dear friends." March 1971.

prolific and productive career of one of show business's greatest professionals are, it seems, about to be written."

Such avid followers of the Sinatra odyssey, led by their president, the authoritative disc jockey Alan Dell, might have been expected to plead with Sinatra: "Stay awhile!" Yet the Society took a firm view that he had made the wisest decision.

"It all sounds a trifle unbelievable," stated the Society, which was formed in 1955. "One can't really comprehend, yet, anyway, the prospect of not scanning the music papers for details of that next LP. Or of hearing about the next Sinatra jaunt. . . .

"It's difficult to imagine that he'll not be in there again, rubbing shoulders with the best (and the worst), continuing to make his vital contribution to the progress of the entertainment world. But the blunt fact is: Frank Sinatra has said, officially, that he's calling it a day. A decision which, at his time of life, is at the least a very wise one. Forget 'I Will Drink the Wine' as a finale. He's still going out proud, with his marbles well and truly in the right place. Maybe not exactly right on top of his game. That finished, surely, in May 1970 [here it was referring to his immaculate British concerts] but certainly at a high level of performance."

Noting that he had undoubtedly been beseeched to change his mind, the Society continued: "We hope, most sincerely, that he doesn't change his mind. That he continues to enjoy his most well-earned retirement. Should the desire to make an infrequent appearance in the recording studio prove too irresistible, then, providing the chops are in working order by all means have a go. . . .

"But please, Frank, don't try the big comeback thing. You did that once before with *From Here to Eternity.* Then, it was the most important thing in your professional career. But, as of now, comebacks are the last thing you want. For even the best champs (remember Joe Louis, Frank?) never come back. NEVER. So resist the selfish clamorings, the over-dramatic pleadings."

Formally thanking him for all the pleasure he had provided, the Society added: "Let's remember you as of now. As we've always (or very nearly always) remembered you: as one of the Great Ones." And with a cynical flourish that now seems to have been unable to take a crystal ball into his future, the Society said: "May we also thank you for retiring now ... and not when you're sixty-five or seventy-five and, in all probability, you might have become a croaking, aging has-been."

His record company marked his exit by sending out a "tribute kit," including a photograph album containing mostly sepia pictures of Frank at work and play; his "final" unfortunate album *Sinatra and Company,* and a statement that said: "Frank Sinatra has been part of all our growing up and he hasn't asked much of any of us, fans, critics, promoters and recording company tap dancers, entrepreneurs and hypesters. No sir, he hasn't asked much. He has given a lot and taken a lot and what we're trying to say is that it is nice to be able to make a move to tell him we really do love him and value him and appreciate him before it's too late. Like, who needs an obituary? Do it before it's too late."

The record company even conducted a series of street interviews with people to get their responses to Sinatra, and included their comments in the package.

In an emotional farewell concert on 13 June 1971 at the Los Angeles Music Center, a huge audience of relatives, show-business personalities and admirers saw a vintage performance. Introduced by Rosalind Russell as "the greatest entertainer of the twentieth century," Frank ran through the musical tapestry of his career, from the Dorsey standards, through the swingers like "The Lady Is a Tramp" and "Fly Me to the Moon," on to "My Way." But he chose what was intended as his final stage song adroitly. Closing with a saloon song that he had projected powerfully for so many years, he smoked a cigarette and sang "Angel Eyes," the song's final line acquiring a freshly emotional quality: "Excuse me while I … disappear." He left the stage and the single spotlight that had focused on him during the song. Symbolically, he did not do an encore. Perhaps he was trying to convince us that, in a wider sense, he would not be back.

"I just want to read Plato and grow petunias," he told reporters. Daughter Nancy remarked that her father considered that the time for retirement was prompted by the fact that it was "the end of an era. And he's right."

A multitude of trophies lined his walls. There were gold discs aplenty, but they came naturally. What were more important to him were humanitarian awards and the many letters of thanks from celebrities and non-celebrities who had cause to thank him for his generosity, which went unnoticed by a press that was happy to expose his temper tantrums and list his personal peccadilloes. From Kennedy to Nixon, he had become the toast of the White House, the living symbol of everything classy and tasteful about the entertainment industry.

Taken aback by the arrival of the new music in the 1950s, Frank had been forced to concede that some of the 1960s music had melodic merit. Sometimes, he would thank the disc jockeys who had given his records airtime "in the middle of Beatle-dom." The arrival of new, gifted songwriters heartened him in the latter half of the 1960s. He was particularly enamored of Jimmy Webb, naming his composition "By the Time I Get to Phoenix" one of the best saloon songs he had ever heard. Sinatra also recorded Webb's "Didn't We" and met the young writer once to encourage him. The quality of songwriters who had grown up alongside Sinatra was proving hard to replace, and men like Webb were sorely needed.

Consulting with conductor Gordon Jenkins during rehearsals for his comeback performance.

While the start of the 1970s marked also the arrival of disco, 1972 provided no trend that was discernible. World events were more profoundly significant. In Vietnam, the last US combat troops prepared to leave. In Ireland, thirteen civilians were shot by British troops in Londonderry on "Bloody Sunday." Richard Nixon regained the Presidency.

Frank sat all this out as a public figure. But a mere two years after his retirement, he was back, just as Bing Crosby had predicted. His first foray, his own TV special in 1973, had as the theme the title of his album, *Ol' Blue Eyes Is Back.*

The voice was more mellow but the stampeding authority of the man carried him through, and, as always, nothing could diminish the power of his phrasing. The mesmerizing strength of Sinatra on stage never relied entirely on the quality of his vocal cords. A whole gamut of his audience's emotions, now stretching back some fifty years, walks on stage with him. His music and those songs were part of our growing up. He does not even have to parade his catalogue of songs for the magic to happen. Thus, his return was not particularly reliant on the tone or power of his voice. What he was able to say and shape with his voice was relevant.

Those "fallow years" that Frank said he sought turned out to be from 1974 to 1980. He has a favorite phrase, saying that he needed to "let some wind blow through my brains," but there was also a sound musical reason. He felt the heavy artillery of rock was not to be challenged, and that, having made a tentative move back into the limelight, he should bide his time, and await better songs than he was hearing from the newer writers.

In those six years, there were no albums. Just before that hiatus, he turned out adequate works called *Some Nice Things I've Missed,* plus a live album from his show called *The Main Event* at Madison Square Garden, New York, on 13 October 1974. There were some dodgy choices on the *Some Nice Things* set. "Tie a Yellow Ribbon Round the Old Oak Tree" and the choppy "Big, Bad Leroy Brown," and even the Neil Diamond smash "Sweet Caroline," were anathema to one with such a depth as Sinatra. What Don Costa and Gordon Jenkins were doing, aiding and abetting such transparently lightweight tracks, is a mystery. The beautiful David Gates composition "If," and Michel Legrand's "What Are You Doing the Rest of Your Life," were the standout items on this weird enterprise. Frank sounded awkward, away from his natural milieu.

But Frank often seemed to have a compulsion to stray into unwise pastures, as if to prove he could rub shoulders with the new movers and shakers. In truth, his greatest strength would have been to remain on his home turf, as the *Duets* albums proved.

If he seemed to mark time professionally in those years, they were attended by events of elation and sadness. He remarried. And then his mother died.

After three marriages, Frank seemed, at sixty, to have settled comfortably into bachelorhood. His career, as it turned out, was not so much concluded

Dolly, the matriarch who actively shaped the future of her only son (here accompanying him to receive an award from the American Friends of the Hebrew University in Jerusalem), died tragically in a plane crash in 1976 en route to Las Vegas to see Frank perform.

as "on hold." Among the ladies he met during his social round was Barbara Marx, former wife of Zeppo, the youngest of the Marx Brothers. Vivacious and composed, the former beauty queen and successful model first met Frank in 1973 and they were married three years later. Accompanying Frank on all his world travels, Barbara, fourteen years younger than Frank, is spoken of by observers as a woman totally suited to his temperament.

Sinatra's wedding in 1976 to Barbara Marx took place at the home of Walter Annenberg, former US ambassador to the Court of St. James's.

While 1976 brought that pleasure, disaster struck in January the next year. Dolly, Frank's mother, died in a plane crash in the snowy mountains of Nevada while en route to see Frank's show in Las Vegas. The stunning blow hit Frank deeply. Coupled with the shocking circumstances of the death was the debt owed to the matriarch who had shaped her only son, encouraged him to pursue his goals and whose dominating personality he had inherited.

Losing his mother, gaining a wife, the mid-1970s was clearly a watershed period for Frank Sinatra. He might have been expected to lie low for a few years, perhaps confining his return to work to a few guest appearances that took his fancy. As if to vanquish his grief, he chose a more active path. It was a dangerous decision. The cynics were lying in wait for him, ready to point out that the man had eaten his words about quitting, and unwisely: his vocal equipment was not what it used to be. Sinatra's timing for a renewal of activity came with some pivotal events, also, on the world stage. In November 1976, Jimmy Carter was elected president of the US, defeating Gerald Ford. Concorde began regular flights that year between London and Washington. On 4 July, the US celebrated the bicentennial of the Declaration of Independence.

By the start of 1977, the rock scene had been hijacked by punk. Safety-pins in their cheeks and ears, punk rockers like the Clash and the Damned and self-described "new wave" artists wrought havoc on the Old Guard of music. The Sex Pistols screeched about "Anarchy" in the UK and a new sound owing more to social change than to making music was polarizing the nation. Since it was rooted more in Britain's social fabric, and rising unemployment figures, the punk movement had only a limited impact on the US, where its more musical partner, dubbed New Wave music, made its mark with groups like the Ramones. For those who, like Frank Sinatra, had lived through the romantic popular music of the 1950s and believed the Beatles and the Rolling Stones to be iconoclasts, the new sound and stance were

A moment of light relief during rehearsals at Carnegie Hall in 1974.

atrocious. There were some beacons of light during these dark days for grown men. Steely Dan brought articulacy to rock. George Benson broke through with *Breezin',* the Eagles with *Hotel California* and Stevie Wonder with *Sir Duke,* his tribute to Duke Ellington, who was another Sinatra friend, and there were notable movies such as *The Godfather* and *One Flew Over the Cuckoo's Nest.* Sinatra's own film career had petered out, with only four movies since the 1960s.

Curiously, at this time of upheaval in the rock scene, Sinatra's re-emergence was warmly greeted by a few of the rock stars who had made their mark in the 1960s. Now aged around thirty, they had been young boys or teenagers when Frank was stretching out in the mid 1950s with radio hits "Love and Marriage," "The Tender Trap" and "Witchcraft." Now, those who understood artistry were beginning to accept him as an elder statesman.

Jimmy Page was among the "new rock" community applauding Frank—a truly revelatory fact. In 1968, the guitarist had formed Led Zeppelin. As well as becoming a monumental success on records and in concerts at the giant arenas around the world, Zeppelin were the totem and progenitor of the important heavy metal rock movement of the 1970s and beyond. His music was loud, but Page drew from a broad canvas and was among the unexpected men sitting spellbound at Sinatra's concerts in London, and playing Frank's albums.

In the mid-1970s, the tide began to turn in Frank's favor, particularly among those who, ten years earlier, had smirked at the mere mention of his name and the era it represented. "I was never interested in Sinatra during the 1960s," recalls Justin Hayward, whose thirty-year-old band the Moody Blues now enjoys the tag of "veteran" just like Frank. "I was part of a generation that thought Sinatra was part of the previous generation. I just couldn't connect with him in the years when rock was coming up and I was part of it."

Then, in 1977, the Moody Blues found themselves managed by the same man as Sinatra. He was Jerry Weintraub, whose glittering stable of artists included Neil Diamond, Bob Dylan, the Carpenters, and John Denver. Accompanying Weintraub to a charity concert Sinatra gave in Los Angeles, Justin Hayward was transfixed. "Until then, I'd dismissed him," says Hayward, composer of the pop classic "Nights in White Satin." "Seeing him on stage, it suddenly clicked and I'd never been so knocked out by any performer in my life. I realized he had that capability that is very, very rare: almost unknown, of being the person in the song he's singing. He's cornered the market in that. Totally." A Sinatra song is in Hayward's all-time top five records. "Whenever I go to my home in the south of France, I play Sinatra singing "Summer Wind." It works so well there. And I play him a lot in my car. His narrative style of storytelling is just unbeatable."

And Rod Stewart, who, when he began as a singer, named Frank Sinatra and Billie Holiday as among his favorite artists, declared upon becoming a success: "I admire someone like Frank Sinatra who has been on top for years and has turned on three generations. Magnificent! In fact, I admire him as a man more than as a singer. He's done it all and when he goes on stage it's not as a museum piece but because people sincerely want to hear him."

When Frank arrived in Britain in March 1977, two months after the death of his mother, word was out that the tragedy had changed him. He was said to be introspective, morose, inconsolably sad. At the Royal Albert Hall, the national anthem began the concert, (in aid of the National Society for the Prevention of Cruelty to Children), and Sinatra's devoted audience, awash with jewelery and furs, settled down to welcome him back.

"Up, Up and Away," sang the Fifth Dimension, opening the evening's music. Then Frank strode on, looking rather more gaunt than yesteryear but soon stamping his individuality on "Night and Day" and a string of familiar love songs. His voice was a little ragged, better in the lower ranges on songs such as "A Foggy Day in London Town," in which guitarist Al Viola played beautifully. "Here's That Rainy Day" followed, with "My Funny Valentine" giving it a close run as the best Sinatra interpretation ever.

After "Embraceable You" came "Send in the Clowns." Although Judy Collins had recorded a pure version of this Stephen Sondheim composition, it was always crafted for the pathos and intensity that only a Sinatra could provide. It was a riveting reading: Frank on stage lit only by two pink spotlights. Bill Miller's piano figures were especially pretty.

After proposing a toast to America's new president, Jimmy Carter, Frank surprised us by singing the Elton John composition, "Sorry (Seems to Be the Hardest Word)." How refreshing it was, after the mundane choices on some of his albums in recent years, to have him choose a fine ballad with poetic lyrics and an unusual melody.

And then came a surprise. "I loathe this song," he exclaimed, before plunging into "My Way." Because it signalled an exit door through which he had returned, the lyrics of the song seemed to bring remorse. This was odd. He had the choice not to sing it; but he seemed to recognize his fans' expectation of the song that was now part of him.

A vibrant "The Lady Is a Tramp" showed that despite the air of melancholy that permeated the show, he still had energy. Then he left the stage. The standing ovation showed that Sinatra devotees were glad he was back.

On British soil, it was a pity he did not feature a Beatles song, since many Lennon–McCartney compositions as well as his chosen "Something" and "Yesterday" would have found a comfortable niche in his repertoire. He could also have ventured beyond his older catalogue. But with such a wealth of classic material to choose from, he knew intuitively what that audience had come to hear. He had reclaimed his crown.

Within a month, a compilation album called *Portrait of Sinatra,* released in Britain, shot to the top of the album best-sellers, staying there for three weeks, ahead of such major rock acts as Fleetwood Mac and Pink Floyd.

No artist of any caliber flourishes and grows without risks and challenges. Nobody ever had to explain that fact to Frank Sinatra. If his young life had not been exactly impoverished, his Hoboken years in a tough environment had prepared him for battles. When Columbia Records dropped him and Capitol gave him that tentative chance in 1952, he matched the tension that engendered by taking a huge gamble fighting for the part of Maggio in *From Here to Eternity.* And while his film career moved at times into a formulaic box-office pattern, his music never did. Singing was always his primary muse.

A team player by the rules of the Harry James and the Tommy Dorsey bands, Frank was always too staunchly individual not to fly away as a soloist. It was a bold decision, destined to work. Other moves during his long career did not, notably the choice of some weak pictures and songs. As a man and, by extension, as an artist, Frank has never been a pipe-and-slippers person like one of his inspirations, Bing Crosby. To hear Frank Sinatra sing has never been to experience a vocalist transmitting a melody and story. It is to hear every aspect of life's experiences: his battle for survival itself; his triumphant return from the precipice; his broken love affairs and eventual happiness; his compassionate espousal of humanitarian causes; his imbroglios with journalists; his fatherhood.

By the time he came back from retirement, cynics portrayed him as a doleful narcissist who could not live without applause. It was an easy charge but it failed to examine the artist within. Above all else, it was his vocal style that was going to be under the microscope and nobody could define the expectations of the Sinatra voice better than Sinatra. He knew what he would be offering the public. It was Sinatra taking a risk again, facing the challenge of age. The lesson from Sinatra is that a life on the edge should nourish, rather than break, inherent talent. In every sphere of art, it was accepted that growth, maturity, and wisdom shone through the evolving painter, actor, saxophonist, producer. A grudging attitude seemed to deny that privilege to Frank Sinatra's field of popular music even though the individual nature of his voice demanded it.

Billy Joel, the brilliantly innovative singer-songwriter-pianist, said to me in 1977, "I think Frank Sinatra is a gutsy guy." He added that he would never want to emulate him, because that was not the function of any artist. But to draw inspiration from Sinatra as something of a role model was no bad thing. In any case, Joel added, Sinatra defied imitation.

Frank disliked the word "comeback" but, since his return to activity in 1974, the emphasis had been on live shows. Triumphant concerts like those at Radio City Music Hall in New York City in October 1978 partly emphasized Frank's absence from records for a whole four years. He had recorded some 1,200 songs, but nothing new was coming.

Some who watched and waited theorized that he had surveyed the shifting sands of rock 'n' roll and decided to stay as a live performer only. At no stage of his career had Sinatra been a quitter: as events unfolded, it was clear that he was merely waiting for the right songs to come along to tempt him to record an album that would mark the start of a new decade.

In the summer of 1979, Sinatra embarked on what was perhaps his boldest move to quash any thought that he had pulled away from making albums. The bold operation was *Trilogy,* a three-album set in which Frank would confront his past, the present and future in songs. It was the brainchild of Sonny Burke, whose production credits with Frank stretched over a dozen albums ranging from Frank's collaborations with Duke Ellington and Jobim right through to *The September of His Years,* a classic.

Vastly experienced as a former arranger for big names such as Joe Venuti, Xavier Cugat, Sam Donahue, Jimmy Dorsey and Gene Krupa, Sonny Burke felt that Frank needed to do something more tangible than merely stab at current material. According to the

Trilogy notes by David McClintick: ". . . it seemed to Burke that Sinatra was selling himself short. By focusing so intently on the current musical scene, Sinatra was ignoring the universality and timelessness of his appeal. Comparing himself with the young artists of today, no matter how popular, was irrelevant. Anybody who had been mesmerizing audiences for forty years should be measuring himself by only one standard—his own—and asking himself only one question: What haven't I sung, old and new, that will enable me to continue to innovate and leave my unique mark?" Frank inspected the concept of the album very carefully before accepting the idea; it was all so utterly new to him, he said, that he wanted to be sure. "They came up to Vegas with a reel to reel tape and it *put me away* when I heard it," he told Sid Mark.

The Past, The Present, The Future, the six sides of the collection that formed *Trilogy,* was another risk for Sinatra. Burke was joined for the project by inventive arrangers whose empathy with Frank's work covered all his styles: Billy May, Don Costa and Gordon Jenkins.

The retrospective segment of the album took care of itself. The challenge was to re-energize old songs and Frank friskily set about "The Song Is You," "Street of Dreams," "My Shining Hour" and the beautiful "More Than You Know" to remind us where he had come from. Billy May's vigor set the seal on Frank's self-conscious dip into his history.

Covering the present was going to be the most rewarding part of the *Trilogy* project. Opening with the pleading "You and Me (We Wanted It All)," written by Carol Bayer Sager and Peter Allen, was a smart move. The song was perfectly tailored for the Sinatra of the 1980s. We wanted it all, he says: passion without pain ... we're not like the best, back when we were dumb, how did we become so smart and learn to break each other's heart? It was a saloon song, a torch song, for the new decade. A song of problematic love that he dispensed with all the power he could muster. Don Costa was at the helm, and there followed Billy Joel's haunting "Just the Way You Are." As David McClintick observed, it would always be tough to improve on such a multi-million-seller, since the original is so ingrained in the head, having been such a monster radio smash. Rather than redo it as a ballad, Sinatra opted for a swinging version enlivened by lots of brass. After six takes, he was satisfied: he rightly deduced that there was no point in repeating the Joel style. It stood in a new frame, vigorously re-defined. Always keen to stay contemporary, Sinatra recorded "Something," the ballad by George Harrison of the Beatles. Considering it "one of the most beautiful love songs written in the past twenty-five years," Frank pointed out that it was also one of the finest songs where a man says I love you to his girl, without her even being present.

Injecting the words with a passion: "Somewhere in her smile she *knows*/That I don't *need* any other lover … you stick around *Jack,* it might show," he said, ad-libbing the name as only he could. The spare accompaniment from Riddle gave the track finesse, and Sinatra went on to perform his favorite Beatles song in his personal appearances.

I cannot think of any other song in which Frank Sinatra has infused as much sincerity and passion as he has on this version of this song. He had originally recorded it in 1970, but the *Trilogy* reading was stunning. His expression of the beautiful, simple song is exceptional, even by Sinatra's standard; and Nelson Riddle's arrangement is exquisite.

After all he had done in forty years, his performance on *Trilogy* was groundbreaking. Nine years earlier, he had "retired." Now he was punching out Jimmy Webb's "MacArthur Park" and the "Theme from New York, New York"—a great Manhattan anthem that sounded as if it could have been written for him at the turning point of his career at the Paramount Theatre: ". . . if I can make it there, I'll make it anywhere."

There were risks, surprises, mistakes. After the intricacy of "Summer Me, Winter Me" (music by Michel Legrand, with lyrics by Marilyn and Alan Bergman), Frank dipped into Neil Diamond's lightweight "Song Sung Blue." The texture of the song, despite a humping arrangement and vocal backing for sixteen singers, just doesn't sit well with Sinatra, who needs rather deeper lyrics.

But ah! Here comes Kris Kristofferson's "For the Good Times," a durable piece of work. Duetting with singer Eileen Farrell, Frank grasps the soul-searching lyrics as if they were his own. And then it's onward to an Elvis Presley song. Hitherto critical of the Presley schtick, Sinatra here relents to a song that Elvis co-wrote with Vera Matson. At his best, on a good ballad, Presley had a rich, pleasing voice … although he was as palpably a country boy from Memphis as Frank was an urban spirit from New Jersey. It showed in their contrasting make-up, and it shows in the comparative

A rare opportunity to relax, here in Monte Carlo. Crosswords absorbed him from an early age, when on film set awaiting his cue. Was this the only attraction of retirement?

readings on this plaintive evergreen. Presley had good pipes. Sinatra, devouring "Love Me Tender" in 1979 at the age of sixty-four, had lived.

Album three, reflections on the future in three tenses, was visionary in concept: a musical fantasy for Sinatra, the Philharmonic Symphony Orchestra and a chorus. This masterwork was composed, arranged and conducted by Gordon Jenkins. The challenge of transporting Sinatra in song via satellite into the future was loaded with danger, laying Sinatra and Jenkins open to charges of pretentiousness. But it became a qualified success.

So ambitious was the narrative content, so demanding on Frank in calling on him to adopt thespian qualities never even needed on the movie set, that there are moments when the dialogue and his delivery sags and drags. Yet it has surprising strengths that are revealed only with patient replays and an open mind. As David McClintick observed: "The work sweeps across the attitudinal and emotional terrain from sage cynicism, to humor, to vulnerability, to childlike wonder." Its themes, from world peace and space travel, suggest a desire by Frank to conduct a symphony orchestra: "I would stand there, big and brave, and say Ladies and Gentlemen, *play* for me, *play* for me."

The overpowering finale, entitled "Before the Music Ends," is self-analytical prose, touching in its glance over the shoulder at his life and work and pleasures. With chorus answering him here and there, Sinatra speaks and sings: he'd reached the age of forty sooner than expected/ living at a fairly hectic pace. The female chorus asks: What will he do now?

A different song must be sung, he answers, when the singer is no longer young. And he needs to do things.... like return to Hoboken "one more time. . . . I want to run down the streets where that thin Italian kid ran/ and slow down at the school/where those nice old ladies tried to teach me/unaware that I knew much more than they did."

"Francis ... don't go home again," pleads the choir. And so it goes on ... following the theme of the title, "Before the Music Ends," he wants to make one more record with the best musicians in the world. "And when that cat with the scythe comes tugging at my sleeve I'll be singing as I leave!"

This was all deeply emotional stuff. It wasn't Sinatra saying farewell again, but examining himself in song. Through his career, he has achieved something rare in the arts, touching the nerve of his audience through his music while earning the respect of the younger set. Strangely, his own moods mirrored those of his audiences, too. The *Trilogy* album was recorded in 1979, the year when Margaret Thatcher became Britain's first woman prime minister, when Egypt and Israel signed a peace accord, when the Ayatollah Khomeini returned to Iran after fourteen years in exile.

At the top of the US and British singles chart that year was a powerful song by Gloria Gaynor called "I Will Survive." In 1980, Frank Sinatra declamatorily showed what survival really meant. It was not a comfortable, cosy album but a seamless suite that joined the past and the present and, with sentiment, vision, and a cutting edge, dared contemplate his future.

The triple album was nominated for six Grammy awards and became a Gold Record within a matter of weeks. Critics were mixed in their reactions but the respected writer Leonard Feather, in the *Los Angeles Times,* considered the enterprise "historic." Sinatra felt that, years ahead, if the critics revisited the album, they might discover its merit.

To his inner circle, for many years, Frank spoke a well-worn slogan: The Best Is Yet to Come. Fifteen full years before the *Duets* operation, *Trilogy* signalled that he was never going to be content to bathe in past glories. Exploration was central to his life.

It was highly symbolic that Frank should have chosen 1980 in which to release such a statement as *Trilogy,* looking at the past, present and future. For if the 1960s and 1970s had found him consolidating his position surrounded by alien forces in music and beyond it, the new decade was much tougher. Both the atmosphere and the reality were more negative and less hopeful at the start of 1980. Unemployment was rising everywhere; in Britain the figure was 2 million and the dreams of the 1960s had been eroded, spiritually and materially. America has always been more generous to its stars, celebrating them as a loveable part of the passing show. In Britain, as Frank prepared for his concerts in September 1980, the young were less enamored of a man who had enjoyed a forty-year run of success, was a millionaire, and in their view should stay at home. Never had rock and popular music been so polarized; one British rock group called itself UB40, which was the number on the nation's unemployment form; the punk revolution had been succeeded by experimental groups whose only ambition seemed to be to topple the status quo.

Sinatra was considered one of the "fat cats." He had it all; his "old-fashioned" music did not stand for anything sociological. At the dawn of a new decade, so the story ran, the popular music scene had to be reinvented. The mold had to be broken, and Sinatra, his kind of music, and everything he stood for in terms of stardom, was to be buried by the young.

It was a generally hostile London into which Frank flew in 1980 for his concerts at both the Royal Festival Hall and Royal Albert Hall, which was nicknamed by his followers the Francis Albert Hall. Here was the difference from his previous visits: while younger writers had observed him as part of their parents' lives, a much more cynical, questioning, aggressive breed of writer was awaiting him in 1980. To them, he represented Old Show Business; they needed to create their own superstars. (The fact that this scarcely happened, and that even now, in the mid-1990s, products of the 1960s largely dominate the rock field, is proof of the creativity and durability of artists of that era.)

In the words of Derek Jewell, Britain's most perceptive writer on popular music, in the *Sunday Times,* Sinatra had "become the keeper of the flame for everyone from, say, forty to eighty. His songs distil the youth, the nostalgia, of millions. He also happens to be the best at it, an artist of colossal stature. He swings, he speaks, he shapes songs like no one else. That is genius." That, Jewell added, was why thousands had fought successfully for tickets for his London fortnight. Sinatra's voice had gradually, inevitably, been declining "although not his mastery of phrasing. He was in better voice than for years. He sang a demanding descending scale without a quaver in 'Strangers in the Night,' as if slyly to celebrate the fact."

The negative view of Sinatra in 1980 was reinforced by his arrival with a retinue of bodyguards who, along with Frank and his wife Barbara, occupied the entire sixth floor of London's Savoy Hotel. Barbara Sinatra's arrival at the House of Commons with a phalanx of bodyguards underscored the great divide. Suddenly, Frank was too flash for comfort.

"It is not easy," wrote James Johnson in the *London Evening Standard,* "to warm towards somebody who apparently likes to cast himself in the role of an arrogant and unpleasant individual off-stage." In that year of 1980, a strangely nihilistic attitude was bearing down on Frank. Commentators were more concerned with the negative reports from the US about his tilts at journalists and others than about his art or, indeed, his survival and growth. Fifteen years later, the same writers and their sons and daughters would be singing a very different tune, applauding the *Duets* album and saying how proud they were to have lived through the history book that was represented by Sinatra.

Fifty thousand people attended Sinatra's London concerts in the year that *Trilogy* was released. A Sinatra show had by now become a rite more than a concert, attended by believers who hung on every note, entirely happy with Frank's replications of songs that had marked their lives.

Even then, there were remarks that his voice had been declining, if not his phrasing. As he strode on stage in his tuxedo, the band silent, to be greeted by a standing ovation, it seemed to me that the world of popular music, which has marked my life, had split. They were never going to build singers like Sinatra any more; and yet it was too soon for the great music of the 1960s and 1970s to be acknowledged. That was to come in the 1990s.

Who, though, could not warm to Frank Sinatra, accompanied by a rich orchestra, crackling his way through "The Lady Is a Tramp" All those taunts that he might have lost his voice were stilled as he sauntered through "Strangers in the Night," which would have exposed any hoarseness; in "I've Got the World on a String," he used his finger as a neat prop during the line that calls for it; and he sang all the songs we wanted. Completing his twenty-one song run that night, he hit upon a theme of compositions about cities, "Chicago," "A Foggy Day (in London Town)" and "New York, New York." He told the audience: "There are only two of us left who do these songs. Bennett and me. I think they're a great part of the English language." It was gratifying to hear him praising Bennett again (how many rock artists are generous on stage to their contemporaries?).

These were the years of Reagan and Thatcher. Frank Sinatra, raised in an actively Democrat house by his party activist mother, seems to have shifted allegiances slightly during his life, from mid-left to mid-right. As with Kennedy, so with Reagan: on 19 January 1981 Frank produced and directed the inaugural gala for Reagan at the White House, constructing a special version of "Nancy (With the Laughing Face)" for the president's wife.

The 1980s were to become a testing time for Sinatra but his supporters grew ever more vocal. President Reagan was inspired to write a letter emphasizing the positive side of the star who courted danger by his public outbursts and who survived by the scope of his genius. "I have known Frank Sinatra for a number of years," the president said. "I am aware of the incidents, highly publicized quarrels with photographers, nightclub scrapes, etc., and I admit it is not a lifestyle I emulate or approve. However, there is a less publicized side to Mr. Sinatra which justice must recognize. I know of no one who has done more in the field of charity than Frank Sinatra."

The singer's establishment of a Frank Sinatra Student Scholarship Fund in his native Hoboken was attended by Reagan in 1984, and Sinatra's charitable gestures continued. In 1981 he went to Buenos Aires where he earned a reported $2 million for four

concerts, most of the money going to various children's homes in Argentina. He raised near-ly $500,000 at a concert given with his old friend Sammy Davis Junior, to provide financial support for a special murder task force in Atlanta, Georgia, where the police authorities were seeking the killer of twenty-one black children. In a London concert, he donated some £50,000 to the St. John's Ambulance Brigade.

Sinatra has always been an involved and astute businessman. He believed quite rightly that his art should be properly rewarded, for there is only one Sinatra. His self-con-fessed interest in the business of entertainment, which peaked in 1962, had ensured that his fees were set to generate a high income. His unashamedly luxurious lifestyle, with homes in Palm Springs and New York, never closed down the outward spirit of the man. He did not retire and close the electric gates behind him like many a millionaire. Few, if any, enter-tainers can match his record in huge, tangible gestures of charity.

As the British writer Benny Green observed in a program note for one of Sinatra's concerts: "What might one deduce from this kind of gallantry? That Sinatra's slum child-hood has never receded into the forgotten past, that it is still very close and very real to him, probably the most vital phase of his entire existence. His philanthropy is not just a quixotic gesture but a sincere attempt to ease some of the pain and suffering which he knows from personal experience to be a commonplace in the world today." Green added that Sinatra's work, at a financial loss, for other people was "unprecedented in the world of entertainment but is entirely consistent with his attitudes throughout his life."

President-elect Ronald Reagan and his wife Nancy are brought to the stage by Sinatra after the inaugural gala honoring them at Washington's Capitol Center in 1981.

Charity for Sinatra was in very short supply when he returned to London, one of his favorite places on earth, for concerts at the Royal Albert Hall from 17 to 22 September 1984. A rising breed of new writers was now harnessed firmly to newspapers that questioned Sinatra's contribution to his era rather than celebrated and welcomed him. Logically, he should have been received as, at the least, a venerable institution. But for so many, the point had to be made: he was "croaky." Sinatra's age apparently disqualified him from going on stage, whether he could fill the Albert Hall with ecstatic fans or not.

For Frank, part of the show must have been like old times, since the opening act was a band in which the youngest musician was twenty-seven. The band was led by the fire-house drummer Buddy Rich, who had partnered Sinatra in the Dorsey band. Don Lusher, whose trombone partnered Frank during the Albert Hall season and went on to Paris and Vienna, where he augmented the Rich band to support Frank, recalls: "Frank's a stickler for tempos, dynamics, feel, intonation and the emotions of his music. Providing everything is right, he is fine to work with. If that is not the case, he will let you know about it and get it put right immediately. I found it absorbing to study his know-how with an audience. He tends to move around the orchestra during a concert so sometimes he is just a yard or so from you." The Princess of Wales attended one of the shows at the Albert Hall, but the mood of London critics was mostly negative.

The winds grow colder ... suddenly you're a lot older, sang Frank Sinatra in 1981. The song was "The Gal That Got Away." Of course he was a lot older, and for those who continued to listen, it was nothing to be concerned about. *She Shot me Down,* the surprising album with that song, was a patchy affair. The album cover finds him, leather-jacketed, glass of Jack Daniel's, cigarette burning, Sinatra enveloped by smoke. The role he's cast in is his favorite mirror image, that of the saloon singer. Yet inside, some of the songs don't do him credit.

What was he doing, even going near a composition like "Bang Bang (My Baby Shot Me Down)?" Written by Sonny Bono and made into a hit by Sonny and Cher, the song had the superficiality that had irritated him when he had been wheeled in that direction at his old record label, Columbia. Even songs like Stephen Sondheim's "Good Thing Going" (from the musical production *Merrily We Roll Along*) and Alec Wilder and Loonis McGlohon's song "South–to a Warmer Place" did not quite measure up to Sinatra's standards. And yet, it was reassuring that he was taking gambles, making what in my view were errors of choice. Music is subjective; doubtless he considered the songs worthy. And the album had magical moments.

Carrying a theme of farewell to a woman who had left him, the album, produced by Don Costa, featured arrangements by Nelson Riddle and Gordon Jenkins. The latter, whose songwriting always veers towards the unorthodox, wrote a particularly fine song for the album, "I Loved Her." "She was Boston, I was Vegas/She was crêpes suzette, I was pie … but I loved her." She was afternoon tea; I was saloon, sang Frank. Could any song have been so cannily crafted for its artist?

"Thanks for the Memory," the Bob Hope signature song, never sounded better than this. Frank invested it with a true poignancy. Two unexpected songs, "I Loved Her" and "Monday Morning Quarterback," carried an aching involvement by the singer. "A Monday morning quarterback … never lost a game," he says of a love affair that went awry. The lyrics, by Pamela Phillips, with melody by Don Costa, sounded dead right for Sinatra's ability to examine his own feelings in song. In 1981, here was Sinatra turning up the heat on one of his best performances. "It's easy to win it when you know you'd never play it quite the same," he sings of the "Monday Morning Quarterback."

Sinatra sings and band leader Harry James plays "All or Nothing At All" in 1979, using the same arrangement they used forty years earlier to catapult Sinatra to fame.

And on a snatch of the song "It Never Entered My Mind," there was the answer to anyone who wanted to criticize him for having a mellower voice. What did that matter, when measured against his enunciation of lines in the song like: "Uneasy in my ... easy chair/ Once you told me I was mistaken that I'd awaken with the sun and order orange juice ...for ... one/it never entered my mind." With merely a tinkling piano behind him, Sinatra was at his best. With Sinatra, you always have to keep listening; were those who were kicking about his toupee, his brawls, and his sagging vocal cords still giving the artist any listening time?

"Where once he climbed inside the skin of a song, he is now content to address it politely like a half-remembered acquaintance," carped Max Bell in *The Times.* In the *Daily Mail,* Baz Bamigboye declared pithily: "At sixty-eight his voice has gone, so for crooner read croaker." Only George Melly, writing in the *Sunday Times,* observed the newish stance of Frank Sinatra, which was clear even to audiences. Writing of Sinatra's "mellow dignity, wryly exploited," Melly said the aggressive stance of yesteryear had been replaced by courtesy, "... even, it would seem, modesty. That dodgy edge, that sense of street-wise menace, has evaporated."

In *People,* John Smith dismissed Frank as: "Bloated and croaky and forgetting his lines ... the magic is gone. Francis Albert is yesterday's man with about as much sex appeal as an old sock." As with some of the biographers who would later vilify Sinatra, such vituperation told more about the author than about the artist. It is all too easy to sit there with a pen sharpened like a razor and exploit the man's weaknesses. The task is to portray, explain and balance what it is about Sinatra and major artists that has attracted millions to his work, then as now.

The sniping of the critics was paralleled by one of the fans, quoted in a British newspaper. Angry at being denied access to her idol as he left the Albert Hall, she said: "We made him a millionaire. He

Savoring the moment with Princess Grace of Monaco and Sophia Loren at Monaco's Red Cross Ball in 1979.

could have treated us better." The implication was that Sinatra somehow owes us something for following his work. This is not so. Put simply, he has something to offer. We buy it. Or we don't.

In London in 1984, students of Frank Sinatra did not see the same man who was being projected in the media as "old and boring." They saw an artist, sixty-eight years of age and not pretending to be anything else, with a worn voice certainly, but his command of popular song entirely intact. Painters, instrumentalists, composers, writers, are allowed to mature and are often praised for displaying a talent enriched by age. Frank Sinatra would have to wait for a further ten years before reaping his due recognition from the tigers of the 1980s.

Sometimes there was a chink of emotion when he spoke on stage to reveal the inner man. In a particularly ebullient mood on 7 November 1991, at his concert at the 20,000-seater Spectrum in Philadelphia, Sinatra paid his respects to his pal, the locally raised Sid Mark, as "one of the best friends I ever had in my life." Frank told the crowd "I have had friends, four or five in my career who have stayed with me when things were dark… I love ya [to Sid]."

"I had a lot of friends," Sinatra jested, "and about three days later, they'd gone. [Laughs.] I ran out of money."

Turning to his songs, he said sardonically: "This is a Rodgers and Hart. You know all of these songs. I don't do anything that's new because there's nothing new. And if it was new, I wouldn't understand the damned thing!" And, twenty years after his proclaimed "retirement," he lampooned himself lightly: "I hope this doesn't come as a severe shock," he told the audience, "but I'm through." The audience moaned: "NO!" Sinatra: "Oh yeah, oh it's boozing time!"

Audience: "ONE MORE!"

Sinatra: "One more what? I'm going to the bar. I'll be saying to the waiter in a minute: One more, please!" That led him into his saloon song, "Angel Eyes": "Hey drink up all of you people … the drink and the laugh's on me."

It's histrionic stuff, but his audience wouldn't want him any other way.

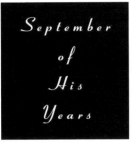

September of His Years

As he considers himself a saloon singer, the choice of venues for him (presumably by promoters rather than by Frank) has been a continual mystery. Any artist of his genre needs a warm setting, and a little intimacy with the audience; in London, the Royal Albert Hall or the Festival Hall should be an extension, for him, of his Savoy Hotel suite. Inexplicably, in July 1990, Frank found himself playing to 9,000 people for £75 a ticket at the dreary London Arena in Docklands, a place more suited to an industrial exhibition. Similarly, many of the cheerless venues he has been playing in the early 1990s in the US were hardly suited to an artist of his genre.

By now old-timers, Dean Martin, Sammy Davis Junior, Shirley Maclaine and Sinatra share the Indian summer of their years.

The aging artist with the compulsion to work, to the delight of his followers, found a mean and tetchy British press accentuating the negative rather than celebrating his presence at the London Arena. Even his opening words to the audience: "I want to lie down," and "Anybody got any smelling salts … there are so many places to play and I'm getting old," were reported as if to rebound on him, rather than in the self-deprecating spirit in which he spoke. In a grudging review in the *Sunday Times,* Richard Cook wrote: "Sinatra can exalt songs and he can destroy them. But since his voice has grown fallible with age he seems to have realized that he can't take chances with the tunes any more, and most of the set found him concentrating hard." Sinatra hardly needs my qualification or excuses but the truisms about the fallibility that came with his seventy-four years, not taking chances and concentrating hard seem to me fairly natural for an artist of his seniority. What can one expect?

There was more from Richard Cook's tetchy pen: "The voice is in a state of grand deterioration. The tremor of his sixties has turned into an omnipresent wobble but the most troubling thing is his inability to sing softly without sounding gruff and throaty. He tends to shout through songs where once he could have glided across their bar lines. . . . where he once let the voice tell the story of the lyric, he now waves his free hand around a lot to embellish meanings. Twice he hushed the orchestra when it was driving him too hard. Frank Junior, who directs the band, is a comforting presence for the old man."

Sinatra *always* waved his arms to lend theater to his songs. A son out front would *naturally* "lend comfort" to his father. One might *expect* a voice to "grow fallible with age." As always, one's reaction depended upon the spirit with which one entered the concert hall. Personally, I went to celebrate the still-powerful artistry of the maestro, and I didn't expect him to be singing "Ring-a-Ding-Ding" with gusto. Sinatra deserved better than the carping about his vocal cords; they long ago ceased to be the vital aspect of his art.

Legend has it that Frank Sinatra once said: "I don't know what it means when people call me a legend. What is a legend? King Arthur is a legend. I can't relate to it."

Defined in *Chambers's 20th Century Dictionary*, legend means "a person having a special place in public esteem because of striking qualities of deeds, real or fictitious; and the body of fact and fiction gathered round such a person." Genius is described as "the special inborn faculty of any individual; special taste or natural disposition; consummate intellectual, creative or other power, more exalted than talent."

Self-effacement has hardly been a lifelong characteristic of Sinatra and yet, particularly in his screen portrayals, he has often assumed the role of the underdog. Nor has it always been the role itself that defined him; that was, and still is, wrapped up in his way of speaking, as opposed to singing. The edge of melancholy in his voice suggests a man not entirely at peace with himself. And there lies the essence of Sinatra's legend or genius that he would never be able to identify, since it is too much a part of his inner self: he is able to transmit his soul through a lyric to which he can relate. It becomes much more than popular singing. It becomes oratory that happens to be set to music.

"I want to lie down— anybody got any smelling salts?" During a sell-out concert in the late 1980s, Liza Minelli provided the rejuvenating support.

"There is a great arrogance about him," observes Don Black, speaking of Sinatra's work. "When he's singing, there's a risk and a danger, which I suppose is what makes a star. A star should be unreachable and untouchable, and you wouldn't want to get too close to him!"

Some of that cocktail he dispenses, a heady mix of great songs and personal swagger, reached a new public in the early 1980s. To call it a renaissance would be to exaggerate, since he had not lost his muse. But after a few years of being considered old hat, he came in for positive reassessment by young adults everywhere.

The reason for this was difficult to detect precisely. It could simply have been the pendulum of taste swinging his way. It could have been, in part, a generation realizing the bankruptcy of its own legacy to music. It could simply have been a whole lot of people playing fair, realizing that the game was up, that Sinatra was a one-off, too good to miss.

The trend gathered speed from around 1983, when *Rolling Stone* magazine, originally the engine-room of counter-culture, included a substantial entry on Sinatra in its *Encyclopedia of Rock and Roll,* a tome and a title that Frank would have cast to the wind at the birth of that music.

Said *Rolling Stone:* "His poised, trombone-like phrasing, his nearly 100 hit singles and his career trajectory—from riot-inducing teen idol to movie star to pop elder statesman—have been the model and envy of rockers from the beginning." It was reassuring that such an acknowledgement of Frank's stature should come from such a bastion of hip journalism, but then the late Ralph J. Gleason, who co-founded the magazine with editor and publisher Jann Wenner in 1966, had long understood that popular music drew from a wide canvas. The new sound of rock would only displace popular music temporarily. When Gleason was the editor of *Jazz* magazine and wrote a column that appeared in the *San Francisco Chronicle* and *Philadelphia Bulletin,* he contributed the notes to Sinatra's quintessential 1959 album *No One Cares.* As always, Gleason brought rare insight and generosity to his writings.

"For all our gaiety and our brass," he said of his native America, "this is a country with an element of sadness running through its soul. The Italians and the Irish, the Jews and yes, even the English, have a melancholy side to their nature and thus we have a great appetite for the song of unrequited love, the lament of love grown cold or hopeless." That underlying element of tragedy was, he insisted, embedded in most American art and life itself. And it was one of the reasons Sinatra could sing sad songs so well.

These truths and the tangible evidence of Sinatra's music percolated through to the collective consciousness of younger artists in the 1980s. This was in direct contrast to the mean reception given to Sinatra by British critics. It was a pleasure to hear Linda Ronstadt, accompanied by Nelson Riddle no less, lend her pleasing voice to a collection of torchy ballads. Carly Simon sang in the genre, too. Both women would become excellent partners for Frank on *Duets* projects, Carly with "Guess I'll Hang My Tears Out to Dry" and "In the Wee Small Hours of the Morning;" Linda with a warm and resonant "Moonlight in Vermont," that song of beauty with no rhyming in its exceptional lyrics. Harry Connick Junior developed a sizeable following and although his offering was more style than content, the affirmation of the beauty of the music and stance of Sinatra was welcome, coming from Connick's generation.

"There is only one role model for us all to follow," Andy Prior told me. The young British singer, born in 1963, has been gathering popularity in recent years with his unmistakable Sinatra vocal style with which he also fronts a full orchestra. Crossing the generations, Prior acts as a fascinating case study of how and why the young have latched on to the music of Sinatra. "Growing up in my teens, I found the simplicity of rock and roll music didn't interest me because to me there was less skill needed to perform it than there was to perform the great songs in the correct manner. I'm still learning; I'll never get it right; I think Frank Sinatra would probably say that, as well."

Andy Prior points out that educating audiences in the truth that his style of music is richer than rock 'n' roll is difficult because "they have got used to rock 'n' roll, where so many other things are going on. The artists dance, wiggle their hips, produce spectacular light shows. It's not enough now to stand alone under a spotlight and sing."

By 1995, Andy Prior had been professional as a singer for sixteen years, with one huge difference aside from age separating him from the formative years of Frank Sinatra. Prior fronts a big band and finds the dual role (akin to Sinatra being Dorsey as well as launching his own career) highly demanding. "I've got to try to be like one of those legendary bandleaders we've all read about, *and* a great singer at the same time. It does get confusing!" But he has won through and notices growing interest in his style of music, an awareness of Sinatra as its originator.

"It's not a nostalgia kick," he says. "Following in Sinatra's steps, or in a bandleader's steps, a lot of people take the easy option and become 'ghost' bands." There are, particularly in Europe, several orchestras which simply try to recreate the music of yesteryear. Prior has chosen a tougher route, acknowledging Sinatra as the model but moving on from his example. With no dance-hall circuit, Prior, as the business manager as well as leading artist, takes his ensemble into major theaters for, say, ten shows a week, reaching 1,200 per performance. "These people are buying Frank Sinatra's albums," he points out, "but they can't go and see him. All right, we're a poor substitute and always will be, but at least it's good, live music and they can see we've worked at it, just like Sinatra did."

Observing, as he travels, the revival of interest in Sinatra and his style of music, Andy Prior says: "Hopefully people are seeing through the garbage they are being thrown. The revival of interest is everywhere. I think it began when 'New York, New York' by Sinatra got into the charts after being played a lot by Terry Wogan [Britain's eminent BBC Radio 2 disc jockey]. The song became an anthem at the end of every disco session the length and breadth of Europe. It spread to the wine bars and the revival gained pace."

Sinatra should never retire, according to this lifelong performer and student of his art. "You can't retire in this business," Andy Prior asserts. "It's your life; it's like saying you're going to stop living. The guy should continue to do what he does best. On the *Duets* albums, I think Sinatra outsings some of the contemporary artists of today who are thirty or forty years younger. He shows he's still the boss. It's a bit like a large cathedral organ that's been there for 500 years. Everybody knows it's had its day really, but it's still nice to hear it. Because you're listening to history."

Sinatra is acutely aware of the shortage of venues in which today's new artists ought to be able to experience the kind of apprenticeship he enjoyed. He says that his grounding in the "years on the bus" with the James and Dorsey bands were his truest education. For nearly 365 days a year, he walked, slept, ate and dreamed about his work. Watching other singers, learning the necessary dynamics of stagecraft, mingling with equally dedicated musicians who understood their craft remains the best method, but a program of education of the public is necessary to make this economically viable. On many American campuses, college bands are prospering, but the reality is that young people are faced with great diversification of choice in music, from rock to country, from soul to jazz. A complex, crowded market place makes a repeat of Sinatra's era difficult, but it is possible for popular music to prosper as part of a wider picture.

The success of the *Duets* albums pinpoints the big difference between the period of live work about which Sinatra and many others become misty-eyed. The making of an album as the first stop for a new artist has overshadowed the touring circuit. In Frank's years with the bands, the concert schedule was the primary activity, with records an important adjunct. That has been reversed in the minds of record companies that today finance artists and think about videos long before significant live performances reach the debate.

In this respect, for Sinatra, the situation has come full circle. For if he had never walked on another stage from 1980 onwards, the recording studio would be his more comfortable home for the rest of his life. For that is where he has always been at his most lethal, where the panoply of his work is evident.

Seizing the upswing in the international attitude to his kind of music, Frank Sinatra's entry into a recording studio in April 1984 was to prove a milestone, even by the standards of his

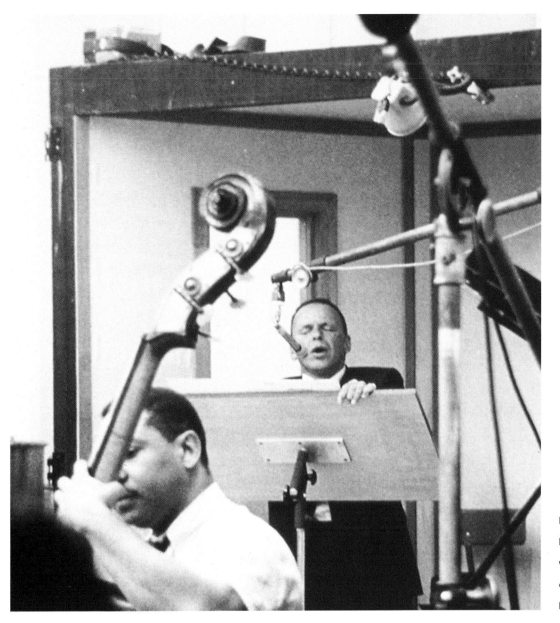

forty-five-year career. The cream of the world's musicians gathered at the A & R Recording Studios in New York, under the production baton of Quincy Jones. The recording engineer was Phil Ramone, who would go on to produce the *Duets* album eleven years later.

In that Manhattan studio, and at other sessions at Ocean Recording Studios and Village Recorders, Los Angeles, in the next month, the goal was to create an historic album. Frank was to be surrounded by the very best from the world of music. Sinatra has always expressed the utmost respect for serious musicianship and the allure of an album by him, produced by the prestigious Quincy, guaranteed the participation of the finest players in the field. Assembled for Frank was a Who's Who of living jazzmen: George Benson on guitar, Lionel Hampton on vibes, Frank Foster and Frank Wess on flute, Ray Brown and Major Holley on bass, Jon Faddis, Joe Newman and Randy Brecker on trumpets, Steve Gadd on drums, Jerome Richardson and Michael Brecker on saxophones, Urbie Green on trombone and many more.

Quincy Jones was certain that being in the company of such gold-carat musicianship, Frank would be inspired. And, in truth, after all he had come through, Frank *needed* to have the ingredient of surprise, and refreshing new musical landscapes, to maintain his interest. His maxim of keeping moving, not going "on repeat," was still holding in 1984 and the idea of the album was to encourage, stimulate, bring out the best in him.

With a small, seated audience that included Michael Jackson, Roberta Flack, Jimmy Webb and Sylvia Syms, the scene was set for what became an album conceived with glamour in mind. It was to be called *L.A. Is My Lady.*

Sinatra did not need to flex his muscles at this stage in his life. The history book could already be written. But, as Louis Armstrong said, a musician does not stop playing; he keeps performing until the very last note. Some do that by pressing the rewind button, demanding applause only for past glories. Sinatra always, but always, strove for growth. To a world in which some theorized he may want to hang up his boots, these sessions would point his future rather than savor the past.

The title track took up Frank's theme of singing about cities: after the praises of New York, Chicago and London it was a diplomatic, as well as celebratory move, to tilt his hat to the city that was his home. Although the song bore lyrics by Marilyn and Alan Bergman and music by Quincy Jones and Peggy Lipton Jones, it lumbered along with little spark and didn't quite carry the same clout as his other city songs. Following this, "The Best of Everything" stepped up the heat, a simple upbeat song that allowed Frank to get into a groove a fraction more.

It was when he switched to the classics that Frank and the band tore away. "Teach Me Tonight," with Sammy Cahn's astute message, was rarely interpreted with such one-to-one impact. Cole Porter's "It's All Right with Me" raced away at a sizzling pace, the band and George Benson's fluent guitar work bouncing Sinatra along. "They're not her chops, but they're so tempting chops," he sings crudely, substituting the word for lips. By such pithy remarks has Sinatra become known, and the offensive descriptions of women as "broads" were not going to be eliminated.

Often, when a song has belonged to another performer, Sinatra has marched in and repossessed it. "Mack the Knife," which Louis Armstrong made his perennial international success, trumpet and all, came in for a particularly fierce attack by Frank. With another sizzling guitar run by George Benson tied to an arrangement by Frank Foster, the track jumped. An especially neat aspect was Frank running through the stars of that session who were alongside him in the studio: "We got George Benson, Newman, Foster/We got the Brecker Brothers and Hamp bringin' up the rear/All those bad cats and more are in this band now/With the greatest sounds you're ever going to hear."

And there was a piece of self-deprecation in the new lyric, Frank singing that Satchmo, Bobby Darin and Ella Fitzgerald had all sung it before him, "with such feeling that Ol' Blue Eyes can't add nothing new."

In the same league of driving songs, "After You've Gone" was delivered with zest. But the album was clinched by its restructuring of songs that were known for slower tempos. Just as Frank had grasped Billy Joel's "Just the Way You Are" and redirected it his own way, he approached the slow standard "If I Should Lose You" with a zesty swing that gave it a new lease of life. The tempo slowed for two beauties, "Until the Real Thing Comes Along" and "A Hundred Years from Today," which his old friend Dean Martin had sung successfully many years before, but now, in Sinatra's hands, they were converted into conversation pieces. In "Hundred Years," he kicked off casually, "*Hey,* don't save your kisses." That's Sinatra; no lyric is unalterable, a dangerous tactic that many songwriters dislike; but the price of having Sinatra stamp a song is that he *will* do it *his way.* It always works for *him,* and that's the whole point. There was an immaculate, waltzing reading of "Stormy Weather," too.

But Frank reached his peak when, the pretty piano of Joe Parnello tinkling behind him, he sang a song he considers one of the very best written in the past quarter-century. "How Do You Keep the Music Playing" could only have had a melody written by the distinctive Michel Legrand. And the lyrics by Marilyn and Alan Bergman, whose songs have brilliantly lit the albums of Frank and of Barbra Streisand and others, added such originality and soul-searching pathos that they would be a hit in anybody's hands. This was the song that Frank had insisted Tony Bennett sing. Bennett's superb version notwithstanding, Frank took hold of it and delivered, as he had always done, from within.

The story is one which Sinatra has dealt with all his life. It is about the challenge of sustaining a relationship, building it, "trying with every day to make it better as it grows." The thoughtful Bergman lyrics seem to have a curious attachment to the very core of Sinatra's art, for they end with the line: "With any luck, then I suppose … the music never ends."

Age, Sinatra has said (once he got all that nonsense about retirement out of his system), did not come into any evaluation of his work. He kept himself in good physical shape, had stopped smoking cigarettes and keeping late hours, and the "reed" was in good fettle. With *L.A. Is My Lady* in 1984, accompanied by musicians and a production team of the highest pedigree, Sinatra was striding forth, after the midstream pause of *Trilogy,* with a splendid album.

It would take more than a clutch of icy reviews from Britain to divert a decision by Frank Sinatra. After that album and the European tour, there was a lull, another period when Frank chose to "let the wind blow through my brains."

He listened, but the mid-1980s level of modern songwriting did not attract him. Having recently recorded golden classics in the company of fine players, the next project would have to be special. Ten years would elapse before *Duets.*

In the interim, the 1980s were marked by a moribund period in the field of modern rock music. While new bands came and went, the field was, and remains, dominated by the superstars who came through the 1960s and early 1970s. The big arenas, and the big record sales, were firmly in the control of young veterans like Elton John, Rod Stewart, Pink Floyd, Eric Clapton, the Rolling Stones, Phil Collins and the Bee Gees. In America, the Eagles made a successful comeback tour. Icons who had died, such as Elvis Presley and Jimi Hendrix and Jim Morrison, seemed to transfix the young more than newer artists.

A tremendous renewal of interest in the legend and the music of the Beatles, plus welcome revisionism of the Carpenters and big sales of their albums, signalled that something was happening.

Into this wide-open scenario came the opening of new clubs playing, live and on record, music in the style of the great ballad singers. Even the clothes being worn echoed a dash of fifties cool as customers from London to New York to Los Angeles decided they would rather visit a supper club and hear Frank Sinatra/Peggy Lee-type music than tough it out in a noisy bar. Straight popular music, as opposed to rock, received its ultimate handshake and endorsement from the eighteen- to twenty-year-olds from the music channel MTV. They invited Tony Bennett to present the Video Music Awards along with a member of the Red Hot Chilli Peppers. And Bennett joined such notables as Paul McCartney, Eric Clapton and Led Zeppelin stars Jimmy Page and Robert Plant in starring in VH-1's prestigious series *Unplugged,* duetting with Elvis Costello and k.d. Lang.

"This is not old music. It's great music," declared Bennett. In Los Angeles, on radio stations such as KXLU, which ran a "Molotov Cocktail Hour," the music enjoyed the spotlight, and clubs such as the Gardenia Rooms on Santa Monica Boulevard, the JP Lounge on Hollywood Boulevard and the Lava Lounge on La Brea echoed the trend.

In London, which had lost the Talk of the Town, its major showplace for this music, in the 1970s, a new mecca was born in 1993. The Green Room at the Café Royal hosted such balladeers as Michael Feinstein, Jimmy Webb, Bobby Short, Eartha Kitt, and Sacha Distel.

Radio One, the rock radio station of the young, found its listening figures plummeting while the adult station Radio Two, which was offering the more nutritious Sinatra, Bennett, Carpenters, Anne Murray, and Olivia Newton-John, climbed steadily. At another venue, London's Pizza on the Park, such standard bearers as Blossom Dearie and Gerard Kenny, singing the classics as well as their own compositions, seated at the piano, drew enthusiastic audiences.

The wheel had turned a few notches, and Sinatra sensed it, even from behind his electrically operated gates in Palm Springs.

Three thousand miles away, in Hoboken, New Jersey, the city's public library features a collection of Sinatra memorabilia, including his birth certificate, located behind glass on the second floor. City residents claim that Sinatra has visited the city occasionally, under cover of darkness. The mayor rightly calls for the establishment of a museum. Some of the singer's old 78 rpm records and a copy of his honorary high school diploma are on show at the City Hall. A street on the waterfront is named after him. But now, quite rightly, the mayor wants to see a proper museum established in the New Jersey city where it all began.

This is logical: Elvis fans have Graceland in Memphis; Liverpool has "The Beatles Story," a permanent exhibition, and roads named after

No longer smoking or keeping late hours, and the reed in good fettle, Sinatra continues to stride forth in the 1980s.

McCartney, Lennon, Harrison, and Starr. Anyone visiting Nashville is immediately aware that this is the country music capital. A Rock 'n' Roll Hall of Fame fêtes the great. Hoboken should certainly be the point of celebration for Sinatra, for not only was he born there but it shaped the spirit with which he imbued his work.

Into the late 1980s, there was nothing of the curator about Sinatra as he set about his work with a zeal and energy that would have exhausted artists not half, but a third, his age. He went back on the road, much to the anguish of some of his keenest admirers.

At London's Royal Albert Hall, in 1992, his followers wondered if this was wise, as he appeared not to have complete control over the proceedings. Sinatra fanciers were whispering that it really was time for him to call it a day.

His appetite for work seemed insatiable, though, as he continued, in his late seventies, to do about 100 shows a year, from Connecticut to Nevada. Though he lacked composure at the Albert Hall, he often regained it on some of his American shows, kicking off energetically with "I've Got the World on a String."

"What Frank Sinatra may have lacked in pure technique the fabled singer all but compensated for with style and yes, graciousness," reported the *Boston Herald* of his concert at the city's Harbor Lights in September 1994.

The paper reported that Sinatra, backed by a thirty-two-piece orchestra led by his son, was "upbeat and beaming for much of the show and had a lower register that rattled and croaked as often as it glided. . . . Sinatra seemed to visibly tire during the latter half of the set when he had the most trouble remembering song titles and lyrics." Frank's show, running for an hour, included all his favorites, from the demanding "My Kind of Town" to "One for My Baby."

In another town, it was said that Sinatra was guided on stage by a tele-prompter to his left, which gave him the words to each song. This "he often either ignored or lost track of." He told the audience: "I hope you will forgive me if I forget a few words. I haven't worked in so long I've forgotten how to do this job."

If he really wanted to test his status as a legend, these 1994 concerts offered him succor and what must have been a spine-tingling feeling when he saw the audience of twenty-somethings, singles and couples, mingling with the more mature who had grown up with his music.

In Cincinnati, the *Post,* noting that it was twenty-five years since "My Way," Woodstock, and the moon landing, reported Frank as "bashful about applause and ovations. 'Isn't that a great song?' he asks after nearly every number." But there was nothing robotic about his shows, it appeared: when he sang Cole Porter, he stated to the crowd: "I wish there were more people who wrote songs like this." And then, moving into compositions by Gershwin, Cahn, Van Heusen, Mercer and Arlen, he added poignantly: "They don't write any songs any more. And I'm sorry because I have to sing the same ones over and over again."

His point about the paucity of good new songs was a sound one, but there was no cause for his apology about singing the old evergreens. Artists in every genre are expected to sing their greatest hits and signature songs, and during his one hour on stage "Witchcraft," "Fly Me to the Moon" and "My Way," seemed mandatory.

Nowhere, the *Cincinnati Post* declared, was the magic of Sinatra more evident than when a young couple, silhouetted in the moonlight, slowdanced to "Fly Me to the Moon" on the concrete walkway at the back of the lawn of the theater as Frank sang.

A resonant note was struck by the *Dallas Morning News* in October 1994, reviewing Frank's concert at the Fair Park Music Hall. "Americans always demand their idols be at their best," said the newspaper. "We don't want to see the flickers of what used to be. We want them at the top of their game. But the rules don't apply to Mr. Sinatra. He doesn't have to be at his best; we just want to see him, singing all those songs that suddenly take on a new and powerful aspect sung by the now frail giant."

Recent shows had been notable for forgotten lines and fainting spells. "You found yourself, without realizing it, holding your breath wondering what was going to happen, hoping he would be good, fearing it would get embarrassing. Then he snapped his fingers ... and he began cruising through 'Come Fly with Me.' And there was that voice. The Voice." While Sinatra's voice was not the instrument it once was ("it cracks, it drones, it slips off some notes, it never quite makes it up to others"), you could still hear the echo of the Voice in his voice. "Mr. Sinatra," concluded the *Dallas Morning News,* "is a living touchstone to the glory that used to be him."

In 1994, Sinatra received yet another of the countless invitations to write his autobiography that came during his life. This time, the suggestion came in a phone call from Jackie Onassis. She was dying, and reaching out to say farewell to many of her friends in a special way.

Though Sinatra had been the victim of scabrous biographies, old and new, he declined this chance to respond with his story of his life for the American publishing giant Doubleday, of which Jackie Onassis was a senior executive. Frank sent her a bouquet and a card that read: "You are America's Queen. God bless you, always." His daughter Tina had produced a two-part television documentary of his life. Nancy had written a book. Sinatra decided the job had been done. He might also have taken the view that the sheer weight of his life's work would be his best response to those who had taunted him; and anyway, as it turned out, the story was far from complete.

And then, on 15 November 1994, came the release of *Duets II.* Since the first volume had sold 5 million copies worldwide at that time, the cynics said then (and have maintained) that the second volume was even more of a marketing ploy than the first. It was, so the story ran, a clever strategic move to pair a giant with a string of strong artists. While the first collection had the element of surprise, the second had some excellent as well as some dubious moments. But music's like that and, on balance, Sinatra and Capitol were correct to seek to prove that the first volume had not been a novelty. Phil Ramone was again the producer and Pat Williams conducted a fifty-four-piece orchestra.

"Patti LaBelle asked for a glass of wine to calm herself, assured that FS would approve," wrote Bill Zehme in the album liner note. Whatever LaBelle needed worked perfectly, because her duet on "Bewitched" was one of the album's highlights. Her range and style and interpolations matched Frank's well, note for note, and she laughed impulsively before duetting immaculately with him on the crucial line: "… The laugh's on me."

Even though Frank's voice wavered a little, he knew how to get the best out of "Moonlight in Vermont." Singing about falling leaves, a sycamore, and telegraph cables that sing down the highway came naturally to him, and the pure, tender vocal of Linda Ronstadt complemented him immaculately. Here was one special duet, in which the singers were empathetic in their goals.

There were some grim moments. It was sacrilege to merge two monumental songs, "How Do You Keep the Music Playing?" and "My Funny Valentine," so that neither sounded good. Frank naturally throwing away a song like "Valentine" while Lorrie Morgan sang the Bergman/Legrand composition produced a contrived fail-

When Sinatra asked the koala's name, after being presented with it by Gold Coast developer Mike Gore, he was told it was "Frank."

ure. Similarly, "Fly Me to the Moon" (with Antonio Carlos Jobim) and "Come Fly with Me" (with Luis Miguel) added zero to both the songs and Sinatra's original versions.

There was the infectious sound of Stevie Wonder kicking off the album with wailing harmonica before Frank was joined by Gladys Knight and Stevie's vocal help on "For Once in My Life"; Jon Secada straining to match Frank's voice on "The Best Is Yet to Come"; Chrissie Hynde indulging herself on "Luck Be a Lady"; Steve Lawrence and Eydie Gormé, the consummate professionals, on "Where or When"; Willie Nelson relaxed and conversational on "A Foggy Day," with Frank displaying real energy on a line that seemed oddly appropriate: "How long, I wonder, will this thing last?"

Lena Horne helped Frank caress "Embraceable You," taken at a seductively slow pace and recreating his own image of himself as the saloon singer; Frank Junior joined him on "My Kind of Town," that salute to Chicago, and showed the similarity of his timbre to that of his father. The finale, "The House I Live In,", paired Frank with the brooding intensity of Neil Diamond, perfect for the fervor of the song. As duettists, they were well matched, Frank achieving as much depth as at any time in his career as he sang about children in the playground, and "all races and religions, that's America to me." If that was his final studio recording, it will have been a warm farewell, for patriotism is ingrained in Sinatra, particularly at this stage in his life.

The rat-pack trio in advance of their last proposed 29-city tour in 1988. Liza Minnelli soon substituted for Dean Martin, who retired with kidney illness, and not long after the tour Sammy Davis Junior succumbed to cancer and died in May 1990.

It was easy for the doubters to discard *Duets II* as a piece of opportunism. It is difficult to accept the theory. He did not need to work on attracting a young audience in 1994, and surely did not need the company of contemporary artists to help him. No, both *Duets* volumes were fitting celebrations and full-circle valedictions. Sinatra would have spotted a phoney project and this was, quite simply, a continuation of the fresh experimentation that had stimulated him. The doubters were dispelled; the answer is in the grooves.

The *Duets* albums will remain controversial among collectors of his work. Since the dog days at Columbia at the outset of his career, Frank had largely avoided duets. The notion of sharing the platform did not seem right for such a boss figure.

But the *Duets* projects were a brilliantly conceived repositioning of his status. Paired alongside the massive talents of Streisand and Minnelli, Diamond and Bennett, Sinatra's position remained impregnable. Artistically and technologically, they duetted with him on his terms: he sang live with the band in Hollywood, while everyone else digitally contributed from Europe, New York or Latin America. And the albums propelled him to an even wider audience. Charles Koppelman, chairman of EMI in North America, notes that Sinatra had established himself with a new generation of fans in addition to "maintaining his legions of loyal admirers." Long before the *Duets* albums, Frank had indeed established a dominion that defied any demographic analysis, for the music he sang and the authority with which he stamped it touched the young, the old and those in between.

If the *Duets* were his recording finale, they served him and his legend honorably. Retirement has not been in his vocabulary, but after his concerts in Japan in December 1994, the betting was that he might well not return to the stage, for the physical strain of stage work seems heavy, particularly since he does not compromise on his musical input.

The undefeated heavyweight champion, after a lifetime of achievement in and out of his chosen field, seems uncharacteristically modest when asked how he would like to be remembered. "I just hope that if I leave anything behind it might be the fact that I tried constantly to have taste in what I did," Frank said in 1992 to American broadcaster Sid Mark. "I just feel that every time I went to bat to do something in my work, I wanted it to be the best," he began. He criticized "performers who shall be nameless, who went on stage and threw it away." He did not understand that: "I figure that if you're going to go to bat at all, you should try to hit the home run every time you get there."

As for his achieving his aim, he was quite modest. Hitting a peak did not always happen for him, "because of the frailties of human nature, whether it may have been a bad throat or being a little impatient on a recording session, and me saying: okay, let's press it anyway." What he had tried to do was take popular music and make it an art, "because I believe popular singing is an art all by itself." He had tried to enunciate the words "so that the listener would know what I was saying"; and he made it his business to understand the lyrics he was dispensing. Singers in the business might "catch on to some of those things," he reflected. "I hope they do. It would be a nice thing to be remembered."

"Ladies and gentlemen," he says at the end of most shows to the accompaniment of the melody of "In the Wee Small Hours," "I wish you everything you want in life, for yourselves and your families, lots of hugging and kissing and sweet dreams. And God Bless."

Opposite: The undefeated heavyweight champion of song. "I wanted to be the best."

1941

Las Vegas Nights
(Paramount)
DIRECTOR: Ralph Murphy
PRODUCED BY: William LeBaron

SINATRA'S NUMBER: "I'll Never Smile Again."

1942

Ship Ahoy
(MGM)
DIRECTOR: Edward Buzzell
PRODUCED BY: Jack Cummings

SINATRA'S NUMBERS: "The Last Call for Love," "On Moonlight Bay."

1943

Reveille with Beverly
(Columbia)
DIRECTOR: Charles Barton
PRODUCED BY: Sam White

SINATRA'S NUMBER: "Night and Day."

1944

Higher and Higher *(RKO)*
DIRECTOR, PRODUCER: Tim Whelan

SINATRA'S NUMBERS: "You Belong in a Love Song," "I Couldn't Sleep a Wink Last Night," "A Lovely Way to Spend an Evening," "The Music Stopped," "I Saw You First," (Jimmy McHugh and Harold Adamson).

Step Lively *(RKO)*
DIRECTOR: Tim Whelan
PRODUCED BY: Robert Fellows

SINATRA'S NUMBERS: "Come Out, Come Out, Wherever You Are," "Where Does Love Begin?," "As Long As There's Music," "Some Other Time" (Jule Styne and Sammy Cahn).

1945

Anchors Aweigh
(MGM)
DIRECTOR: George Sidney
PRODUCED BY: Joe Pasternak

SINATRA'S NUMBERS: "We Hate to Leave," "What Makes the Sunset?," "The Charm of You," "I Begged Her," "I Fall in Love Too Easily" (Jule Styne and Sammy Kahn), Brahms's "Lullaby."

The House I Live In
(RKO)
DIRECTOR: Mervyn LeRoy
PRODUCED BY: Frank Ross

SINATRA'S NUMBERS: "If You are But a Dream" (Nathan J. Bonx, Jack Fulton, Moe Jaffe), "The House I Live In" (Earl Robinson, Lewis Allan).

1946

Till the Clouds Roll By
(MGM)
DIRECTOR: Richard Whorf
PRODUCED BY: Arthur Freed

SINATRA'S NUMBER: "Ol' Man River" (Jerome Kern and Oscar Hammerstein II).

1947

It Happened in Brooklyn
DIRECTOR: Richard Whorf
PRODUCED BY: Jack Cummings

SINATRA'S NUMBERS: "Brooklyn Bridge," "I Believe," "Time after Time," "The Song's Gotta Come from the Heart," "It's the Same Old Dream" (Jule Styne and Sammy Kahn), "La Ci Darem la Mano" (Mozart), "Black Eyes" (Russian).

1948

The Miracle of the Bells *(RKO)*
DIRECTOR: Irving Pichel
PRODUCED BY: Jesse L. Lasky,
Walter MacEwan

SINATRA'S NUMBER: "Ever Homeward" (Kasimierz Lubomirski, Jule Styne and Sammy Kahn).

The Kissing Bandit *(MGM)*
DIRECTOR: Laslo Benedek
PRODUCED BY: Joe Pasternak

SINATRA'S NUMBERS: "What's Wrong With Me?," "If I Steal a Kiss," "Senorita" (Nacio Herb Brown and Edward Heyman), "Siesta" (Nacio Herb Brown and Herb Brent).

1949

Take Me Out to the Ball Game
(Everybody's Cheering U.K.)
(MGM)
DIRECTOR: Busby Berkeley
PRODUCED BY: Arthur Freed

SINATRA'S NUMBERS: "Take Me Out to the Ball Game" (Albert von Tilzer and Jack Norworth), "Yes, Indeedy," "O'Brien to Ryan to Goldberg," "The Right Girl for Me," "It's Fate, Baby, It's Fate"(Roger Edens, Betty Comden and Adolph Green), "Strictly USA" (Roger Edens).

On the Town *(MGM)*
DIRECTORS: Gene Kelly, Stanley Donen
PRODUCED BY: Arthur Freed

SINATRA'S NUMBERS: "New York, New York," "Come Up to My Place" (Leonard Bernstein, Adolph Green and Betty Comden), "You're Awful," "On the Town," "Count on Me" (Roger Edens, Adolph Green and Betty Comden).

1951

Double Dynamite (*RKO*)
DIRECTOR: Irving Cummings
PRODUCED BY: Irving Cummings Jr

SINATRA'S NUMBERS: *"Kisses and Tears," "It's Only Money" (Jule Styne and Sammy Kahn).*

Meet Danny Wilson
(*Universal-International*)
DIRECTOR: Joseph Pevney
PRODUCED BY: Leonard Goldstein

SINATRA'S NUMBERS: *"You're a Sweetheart" (Jimmy McHugh and Harold Adamson), "Lonesome Man Blues" (Sy Oliver), "She's Funny That Way" (Richard Whiting and Neil Moret), "A Good Man is Hard to Find" (Eddie Green), "That Old Black Magic" (Harold Arlen and Johnney Mercer), "When You're Smiling" (Mark Fisher, Joe Goodwin and Larry Shay), "All of Me" (Seymour Simons and Gerald Marks), "I've Got a Crush on You" (George and Ira Gershwin), "How Deep is the Ocean?" (Irving Berlin).*

1953

From Here to Eternity (*Columbia*)
DIRECTOR: Fred Zinnemann
PRODUCED BY: Buddy Adler

1954

Suddenly (*United Artists*)
DIRECTOR: Lewis Allen
PRODUCED BY: Robert Bassler

1955

Young at Heart (*Warner*)
DIRECTOR: Gordon Douglas
PRODUCED BY: Harry Blanke

SINATRA'S NUMBERS: *"Young at Heart" (Johnny Richards and Carolyn Leigh), "Someone to Watch Over Me" (George and Ira Gershwin), "Just One of Those Things" (Cole Porter), "One for My Baby" (Harold Arlen and Johnny Mercer), "You, My Love" (Mack Gordon and James van Heusen).*

Not as a Stranger (*United Artists*)
DIRECTOR, PRODUCER: Stanley Kramer

The Tender Trap (*MGM*)
DIRECTOR: Charles Walters
PRODUCED BY: Lawrence Weingarten
SINATRA'S NUMBER: *"Love is the Tender Trap" (James van Heusen and Sammy Cahn).*

Guys and Dolls (*MGM*)
DIRECTOR: Joseph L. Mankiewicz
PRODUCED BY: Samuel Goldwyn

SINATRA'S NUMBERS: *"The Oldest Established Floating Crap Game in New York," "Guys and Dolls," "Adelaide," "Sue Me."*

The Man with the Golden Arm
(*United Artists*)
DIRECTOR, PRODUCER: Otto Preminger

1956

Meet Me in Las Vegas (Viva Las Vegas! UK) (*MGM*)
DIRECTOR: Roy Rowland
PRODUCED BY: Joe Pasternak

Johnny Concho (*United Artists*)
DIRECTOR: Don McGuire
PRODUCED BY: Frank Sinatra

High Society (*MGM*)
DIRECTOR: Charles Walters
PRODUCED BY: Sol C. Siegel

SINATRA'S NUMBERS: *"Who Wants to be a Millionaire?," "You"re Sensational," "Well, Did You Evah?," "Mind If I Make Love to You?" (Cole Porter).*

Around the World in Eighty Days
(*United Artists*)
DIRECTOR: Michael Anderson
PRODUCED BY: Michael Todd

1957

The Pride and the Passion
(*United Artists*)
DIRECTOR, PRODUCER: Stanely Kramer

The Joker is Wild (*Paramount*)
DIRECTOR: Charles Vidor
PRODUCED BY: Samuel J. Briskin

SINATRA'S NUMBERS: *"I Cried for You" (Arthur Freed, Gus Arnheim, Abe Lyman), "If I Could be with You" (Jimmy Johnson and Harry Creamer), "Chicago" (Fred Eisber), "All the Way" (James van Heusen and Sammy Cahn).*

Pal Joey (*Columbia*)
DIRECTOR: George Sidney
PRODUCED BY: Fred Kohlmar

SINATRA'S NUMBERS: *"I Didn't Know What Time It Was," "There's a Small Hotel," "I Could Write a Book," " The Lady is a Tramp," "Bewitched, Bothered and Bewildered," "What Do I Care for a Dame?" (Rodgers and Hart).*

1958

Kings Go Forth (*United Artists*)
DIRECTOR: Delmer Daves
PRODUCED BY: Frank Ross

Some Came Running (*MGM*)
DIRECTOR: Vincente Minnelli
PRODUCED BY: Sol C. Spiegel

1959

A Hole in the Head
(*United Artists*)
DIRECTOR, PRODUCER: Frank Capra
SINATRA'S NUMBERS: "All My Tomorrows,"
"High Hopes" (James van Heusen and
Sammy Cahn).

Never So Few (*MGM*)
DIRECTOR: John Sturges
PRODUCED BY: Edmund Grainger

1960

Can-Can (*Twentieth Century-Fox*)
DIRECTOR: Walter Lang
PRODUCED BY: Jack Cummings
SINATRA'S NUMBERS: "I Love Paris," "C'est
Magnifique," "Let's Do It," "It's All Right with
Me" (Cole Porter).

Ocean's Eleven (*Warner*)
DIRECTOR, PRODUCER: Lewis Milestone

Pepe (*Columbia*)
DIRECTOR, PRODUCER: George Sidney

1961

The Devil at Four O'Clock (*Columbia*)
DIRECTOR: Mervyn LeRoy
PRODUCED BY: Fred Kohlmar

1962

Sergeants Three (*United Artists*)
DIRECTOR: John Sturges
PRODUCED BY: Frank Sinatra

The Road to Hong Kong (*United Artists*)
DIRECTOR: Norman Panama
PRODUCED BY: Melvin Frank

The Manchurian Candidate
(*United Artists*)
DIRECTOR: John Frankenheimer
PRODUCED BY: George Axelrod, John
Frankenheimer

1963

Come Blow Your Horn (*Paramount*)
DIRECTOR: Bud Yorkin
PRODUCED BY: Norman Lear, Bud Yorkin
SINATRA'S NUMBERS: "Come Blow Your
Horn" (James van Heusen and Sammy Cahn).

The List of Adrian Messenger
(*Universal*)
DIRECTOR: John Huston
PRODUCED BY: Edward Lewis

1964

4 for Texas (*Warner*)
DIRECTOR, PRODUCER: Robert Aldrich

Robin and the Seven Hoods (*Warner*)
DIRECTOR: Gordon Douglas
PRODUCED BY: Frank Sinatra
SINATRA'S NUMBERS "My Kind of Town,"
"Style," "Mr Booze," "Don't Be a Do-Badder"
(James van Heusen and Sammy Cahn).

1965

None But the Brave (*Warner*)
DIRECTOR, PRODUCER: Frank Sinatra

Von Ryan's Express
(*Twentieth Century-Fox*)
DIRECTOR: Mark Robson
PRODUCED BY: Saul David

Marriage on the Rocks (*Warner*)
DIRECTOR: Jack Donohue
PRODUCED BY: William H. Daniels

1966

Cast a Giant Shadow
(*United Artists*)
DIRECTOR, PRODUCER: Melville Shavelson

The Oscar (*Embassy*)
DIRECTOR: Russell Rouse
PRODUCED BY: Clarence Greene

Assault on a Queen
(*Paramount*)
DIRECTOR: Jack Donohue
PRODUCED BY: William Goetz

1967

The Naked Runner (*Warner*)
DIRECTOR: Sidney J. Furie
PRODUCED BY: Brad Dexter

Tony Rome (*Twentieth Century-Fox*)
DIRECTOR: Gordon Douglas
PRODUCED BY: Aaron Rosenberg

1968

The Detective
(*Twentieth Century-Fox*)
DIRECTOR: Gordon Douglas
PRODUCED BY: Aaron Rosenberg

Lady in Cement
(*Twentieth Century-Fox*)
DIRECTOR: Gordon Douglas
PRODUCED BY: Aaron Rosenberg

1970

Dirty Magee (*MGM*)
DIRECTOR, PRODUCER: Burt Kennedy

1977

Contract on Cherry Street
(*Columbia*)
DIRECTOR: William A. Graham
PRODUCED BY: Hugh Benson

1980

The First Deadly Sin
(*Filmways/Artanis/Cinema Seven*)
DIRECTOR: Brian G. Hutton
PRODUCED BY: George Pappas, Mark Shanker

by John Ridgway

The following list of Compact Discs will provide the collector with the bulk of the important Sinatra recordings in all periods without too much duplication.

All the discs are readily available in Europe and the USA.

1 9 3 9

With Harry James (on Columbia)

HARRY JAMES AND HIS ORCHESTRA FEATURING FRANK SINATRA - THE COMPLETE RECORDINGS CK66377
21 titles including: From The Bottom Of My Heart/My Buddy/Melancholy Mood/It's Funny To Everyone But Me/Here Comes The Night/All Or Nothing At All/On A Little Street In Singapore

1 9 4 0 – 1 9 4 2

With Tommy Dorsey (on RCA)

THE SONG IS YOU (5CD set) 66353-2
120 titles including: The Sky Fell Down/Too Romantic/ Shake Down The Stars/Moments In The Moonlight/I'll Be Seeing You/Say It/ Polka Dots And Moonbeams/The Fable Of The Rose/This Is The Beginning Of The End/Hear My Song, Violetta/ Fools Rush In/Devil May Care/April Played The Fiddle/ I Haven't The Time To Be A Millionaire/ Imagination/Yours Is My Heart Alone/ You're Lonely And I'm Lonely/ East Of The Sun/Head On My Pillow/ It's A Lovely Day Tomorrow/I'll Never Smile Again/All This And Heaven Too/Where Do You Keep Your Heart?/Whispering/Trade Winds/ The One I Love/The Call Of The Canyon/Love Lies/ I Could Make You Care/The World Is In My Arms/Our Love Affair/Looking For Yesterday/ Tell Me At Midnight/We Three/ When You Awake/Anything/Shadows On The Sand/You're Breaking My Heart All Over Again/I'd Know You Anywhere/ Do You Know Why?/Not So Long Ago/ Stardust/Oh, Look At Me Now/You Might Have Belonged To Another/You Lucky People, You/It's Always You/I Tried

1 9 4 3 – 1 9 5 2

With Columbia Records

THE COLUMBIA YEARS
(12CD box set) CXK 48673
285 titles including: Close To You/You'll Never Know/Sunday, Monday Or Always/ If You Please/People Will Say We're In Love/Oh What A Beautiful Mornin'/ I Couldn't Sleep A Wink Last Night/ A Lovely Way To Spend An Evening/ The Music Stopped/If You Are But A Dream/Saturday Night/There's No You/White Christmas/I Dream Of You/I Begged Her/What Makes The Sunset/I Fall In Love Too Easily/Nancy/ Cradle Song/Ol' Man River/Stormy Weather/The Charm Of You/ Embraceable You/When Your Lover Has Gone/Kiss Me Again/She's Funny That Way/My Melancholy Baby/Where Or When?/All The Things You Are/Mighty Lak' A Rose/I Should Care/Homesick, That's All/Dream/A Friend Of Yours/ Put Your Dreams Away/Over The Rainbow/You'll Never Walk Alone/ If I Loved You/Lily Belle/Don't Forget Tonight Tomorrow/I've Got A Home In The Rock/Jesus Is A Rock In The Weary Land/Stars In Your Eyes/ My Shawl

1 9 5 3 – 1 9 6 2

With Capitol Records

IN THE WEE SMALL HOURS 96826-2
16 titles including: In The Wee Small Hours/Mood Indigo/ Glad To Be Unhappy/ I Get Along Without You Very Well/Deep In A Dream/I See Your Face Before Me/ Can't We Be Friends/Ill Wind

SONGS FOR YOUNG LOVERS 48470-2
16 titles including: My Funny Valentine/The Girl Next Door/A Foggy Day/Like Someone In Love/I Get A Kick Out Of You/Little Girl Blue/They Can't Take That Away From Me/Taking A Chance On Love

SONGS FOR SWINGIN' LOVERS 46570-2
15 titles including: You Make Me Feel So Young/It Happened In Monterey/You're Getting To Be A Habit With Me/You Brought A New Kind Of Love To Me/Too Marvelous For Words/Old Devil Moon

CLOSE TO YOU AND MORE 46572-2
15 titles including: Close To You/P.S. I Love You/Love Locked Out/Everything Happens To Me/It's Easy To Remember/Don't Like Goodbyes/With Every Breath I Take/ Blame It On My Youth

A SWINGIN' AFFAIR! 94518-2
16 titles including: Night And Day/I Wish I Were In Love Again/I Got Plenty O' Nuttin'/ I Guess I'll Have To Change My Plan/Nice Work If You Can Get It/Stars Fell On Alabama/No One Ever Tells You

WHERE ARE YOU? 91209-2
16 titles including: Where Are You?/The Night We Called It A Day/I Cover The Waterfront/

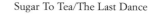

Maybe You'll Be There/Laura/Lonely Town/Autumn Leaves/I'm A Fool To Want You/I Think Of You/Rain

A JOLLY CHRISTMAS 48329-2
14 titles including: Jingle Bells/The Christmas Song/ Mistletoe and Holly/I'll Be Home For Christmas/The Christmas Waltz/Have Yourself A Merry Little Christmas/ The First Noel/Hark, The Herald Angels Sing

COME FLY WITH ME 48469-2
15 titles including: Come Fly With Me/ Around The World/ Isle Of Capri/Moonlight In Vermont/ Autumn In New York/On The Road To Mandalay/Let's Get Away From It All/ April In Paris/London By Night

ONLY THE LONELY 48471-2
14 titles including: Only The Lonely/Angel Eyes/What's New?/It's A Lonesome Old Town/Willow Weep For Me/Goodbye/Blues In The Night/Guess I'll Hang My Tears Out To Dry/Ebb Tide/Spring Is Here

COME DANCE WITH ME 48468-2
16 titles including: Come Dance With Me/Something's Gotta Give/Just In Time/Dancing In The Dark/Too Close For Comfort/I Could Have Danced All Night/ Saturday Night/Day In, Day Out

NO ONE CARES 94519-2
15 titles including: When No One Cares/ A Cottage For Sale/ Stormy Weather/Where Do You Go?/I Don't Stand A Ghost Of A Chance With You/ Here's That Rainy Day/I Can't Get Started/Why Try To Change Me Now?

NICE 'N' EASY 96827-2
16 titles including: Nice 'N' Easy/That Old Feeling/How Deep Is The Ocean/I've Got A Crush On You/You Go To My Head/Fools Rush In/Nevertheless/She's Funny That Way/Try A Little Tenderness

SWINGIN' SESSION! 46573-2
15 titles including: When You're Smiling/

Blue Moon/S'posin'/It All Depends On You/It's Only A Paper Moon/My Blue Heaven/ Should I/September In The Rain/ Always/Hidden Persuasion

COME SWING WITH ME 94520-2
17 titles including: Day By Day/Sentimental Journey/ Almost Like Being In Love/ Five Minutes More/American Beauty Rose/ Yes, Indeed/On The Sunny Side Of The Street/That Old Black Magic

POINT OF NO RETURN 48334-2
16 titles including: When The World Was Young/I'll Remember April/September Song/ A Million Dreams Ago/I'll See You Again/There Will Never Be Another You/Somewhere Along The Way

1960 – 1988

With Reprise Records
RING-A-DING DING 27017-2
15 titles including: Ring-A-Ding Ding/Let's Fall In Love/ Be Careful, It's My Heart/ A Foggy Day/A Fine Romance/In The Still Of The Night/The Coffee Song/When I Take My

Sugar To Tea/The Last Dance

SINATRA SWINGS 1002-2
12 titles including: Falling In Love With Love/The Curse Of An Aching Heart/Don't Cry Joe/ Please Don't Talk About Me When I'm Gone/Love Walked In/Granada/I Never Knew/Don't Be That Way

I REMEMBER TOMMY 45267-2
14 titles including: I'm Getting Sentimental Over You/ Imagination/There Are Such Things/ East Of The Sun/Daybreak/Without A Song/I'll Be Seeing You/Take Me/ It's Always You

SINATRA & STRINGS 27020-2
12 titles including: I Hadn't Anyone Till You/Night And Day/Misty/Stardust/Come Rain Or Come Shine/It Might As Well Be Spring/Prisoner Of Love/That's All/ Yesterdays/As You Desire Me

SWINGIN' BRASS 27021-2
14 titles including: Goody Goody/They Can't Take That Away From Me/At Long Last Love/I'm Beginning To See The Light/Don'cha Go 'Way Mad/I Get A Kick Out Of You/ Tangerine/Ain't She Sweet/ I Love You

SINATRA SINGS GREAT SONGS FROM GREAT BRITAIN 45219-2
11 titles including: The Very Thought Of You/We'll Gather Lilacs In The Spring/If I Had You/Now Is The Hour/The Gypsy/Roses Of Picardy/ A Nightingale Sang In Berkeley Square/ A Garden In The Rain/London By Night

ALL ALONE 27022-2
12 titles including: All Alone/The Girl Next Door/Are You Lonesome Tonight/Charmaine/What'll I Do/When I Lost You/Oh, How I Miss You Tonight/ Indiscreet/Remember/ Together/ The Song Is Ended

SINATRA-BASIE 1008-2

10 titles including: Pennies From Heaven/Please Be Kind/ The Tender Trap/Looking At The World Thru Rose Colored Glasses/My Kind Of Girl/I Only Have Eyes For You/ Nice Work If You Can Get It

THE CONCERT SINATRA 1009-2

8 titles: I Have Dreamed/My Heart Stood Still/Lost In The Stars/Ol' Man River/ You'll Never Walk Alone/Bewitched/ This Nearly Was Mine/Soliloquy

SINATRA'S SINATRA 1010-2

12 titles including: I've Got You Under My Skin/In The Wee Small Hours Of The Morning/ The Second Time Around/Nancy/ Witchcraft/Young At Heart/All The Way/Pocketful Of Miracles

ACADEMY AWARD WINNERS 1011-2

11 titles including: Days Of Wine And Roses/Moon River/The Way You Look Tonight/Three Coins In The Fountain/In The Cool Cool Cool Of The Evening/Secret Love/Swinging On A Star/It Might As Well Be Spring

IT MIGHT AS WELL BE SWING 1012-2

10 titles including: Fly Me To The Moon/ I Wish You Love/ I Believe In You/More/ I Can't Stop Loving You/Hello, Dolly/I Wanna Be Around/The Best Is Yet To Come/The Good Life

SOFTLY AS I LEAVE YOU 1013-2

12 titles including: Emily/Here's To The Losers/Dear Heart/Come Blow Your Horn/Love Isn't Just For The Young/I Can't Believe I'm Losing You/Pass Me By/ Softly As I Leave You/Available

SEPTEMBER OF MY YEARS 1014-2

13 titles including: The September Of My Years/How Old Am I?/Don't Wait Too Long/ It Gets Lonely Early/This Is All I Ask/Last Night When We Were Young/The Man In

The Looking Glass/I See It Now

MY KIND OF BROADWAY 1015-2

11 titles including: Ev'rybody Has The Right To Be Wrong/Golden Moment/Luck Be A Lady/ Lost In The Stars/Hello, Dolly/I'll Only Miss Her When I Think Of Her/ They Can't Take That Away From Me

A MAN AND HIS MUSIC (2CD set) 1016-2

CD1, 13 titles including: Put Your Dreams Away/All Or Nothing At All/I'll Never Smile Again/There Are Such Things/I'll Be Seeing You/ The One I Love Belongs To Somebody Else/The House I Live In

A MAN AND HIS MUSIC 1016-2

CD2, 19 titles including: Come Fly With Me/How Little We Know/Learnin' The Blues/In The Wee Small Hours Of The Morning/Young At Heart/Witchcraft/All The Way/Love And Marriage/Luck Be A Lady

STRANGERS IN THE NIGHT 1017-2

10 titles including: Strangers In The Night/Summer Wind/ All Or Nothing At All/Call Me/ You're Driving Me Crazy/On A Clear Day/My Baby Just Cares For Me/ Downtown/Yes Sir, That's My Baby

MOONLIGHT SINATRA 1018-2

10 titles including: Moonlight Becomes You/Moon Song/ Moonlight Serenade/ Reaching For The Moon/I Wished On The Moon/Oh, You Crazy Moon/The Moon Got In My Eyes/ Moonlight Mood/Moon Love

SINATRA AT THE SANDS WITH COUNT BASIE 1019-2

21 titles including: Come Fly With Me/I've Got A Crush On You/I've Got You Under My Skin/ The Shadow Of Your Smile/Street Of Dreams/One For My Baby/Fly Me To The Moon/You Make Me Feel So Young

THAT'S LIFE 1020-2

10 titles including: That's Life/I Will Wait For You/ Somewhere My Love/Sand And Sea/ What Now, My Love?/Winchester Cathedral/Give Her Love/Tell Her/ The Impossible Dream

FRANCIS ALBERT SINATRA & ANTONIO CARLOS JOBIM 1021-2

10 titles including: The Girl From Ipanema/Dindi/Change Partners/Quiet Nights Of Quiet Stars/ Meditation/If You Never Come To Me/ How Insensitive/I Concentrate On You/Baubles, Bangles And Beads

THE WORLD WE KNEW 1022-2

10 titles: The World We Knew/Somethin' Stupid/ This Is My Love/Born Free/Don't Sleep In The Subway/This Town/This Is My Song/You Are There/Drinking Again/Some Enchanted Evening

FRANCIS A. & EDWARD K. 1024-2

8 titles: Follow Me/Sunny/All I Need Is
The Girl/Indian Summer/I Like The
Sunrise/Yellow Days/Poor Butterfly/
Come Back To Me

FRANK SINATRA'S GREATEST HITS 2274-2

12 titles including: Strangers In The
Night/Summer Wind/ It Was A Very Good
Year/Somewhere In Your Heart/Forget
Domani/ Somethin' Stupid/That's Life/Tell
Her/The World We Knew/This Town

THE SINATRA CHRISTMAS ALBUM 45743-2

13 titles including: Have Yourself A Merry
Little Christmas/An Old Fashioned
Christmas/I Heard The Bells On Christmas
Day/The Little Drummer Boy/Go Tell It On
The Mountain

CYCLES 1027-2

10 titles including: Rain In My Heart/From
Both Sides Now/Little Green Apples/Pretty
Colors/Cycles/Wandering/By The Time I Get
To Phoenix/Moody River/My Way Of
Life/Gentle On My Mind

MY WAY 1029-2

10 titles: Watch What Happens/Didn't We?/
Hallelujah, I Love Her So/Yesterday/ All My
Tomorrows/My Way/A Day In The Life Of A
Fool/For Once In My Life/If You Go
Away/Mrs. Robinson

A MAN ALONE 1030-2

12 titles including: A Man Alone/Night/
I've Been To Town/From Promise To
Promise/The Single Man/The Beautiful
Strangers/ Lonesome Cities/Love's Been Good
To Me/Empty Is/Out Beyond The Window

WATERTOWN 45689-2

11 titles: Watertown/Goodbye/For A While/
Michael & Peter/I Would Be In Love/
Elizabeth/What A Funny Girl/What's Now Is
Now/She Says/The Train/Lady Day

SINATRA & COMPANY 1033-2

14 titles including: Drinking Water/Someone
To Light Up My Life/Triste/Don't Ever Go
Away/ This Happy Madness/Wave/One Note
Samba/I Will Drink The Wine/Close To
You/Sunrise In The Morning

GREATEST HITS VOLUME 2 2275-2

11 titles: My Way/A Man Alone/Cycles/
Bein' Green/Love's Been Good To Me/
I'm Not Afraid/Goin' Out Of My Head/
Something/What's Now Is Now/Star/ The
September Of My Years

OL' BLUE EYES IS BACK 2155-2

9 titles: You Will Be My Music/You're So
Right/Winners/Nobody Wins/Send In
The Clowns/ Dream Away/Let Me Try
Again/There Used To Be A Ballpark/Noah

SOME NICE THINGS I'VE MISSED 2195-2

10 titles including: You Turned My World
Around/Sweet Caroline/The Summer
Knows/I'm Gonna Make It All The Way/
Tie A Yellow Ribbon/ Satisfy Me One More
Time/If/You Are The Sunshine Of My
Life/Bad Bad Leroy Brown/

THE MAIN EVENT 2207-2

12 titles including: The Lady Is A Tramp/
I Get A Kick Out Of You/Let Me Try
Again/Autumn In New York/I've Got You
Under My Skin/ Bad Bad Leroy Brown/Angel
Eyes/ You Are The Sunshine Of My Life

TRILOGY (2CD set) 2300-2

CD1, 20 titles including: The Song Is You/
But Not For Me/I Had The Craziest Dream/It
Had To Be You/ Let's Face The Music And
Dance/ Street Of Dreams/My Shining Hour/
All Of You/More Than You Know

TRILOGY 2300-2

CD2, 6 titles: What Time Does The Next
Miracle Leave?/ World War None/The
Future/I've Been There/Song Without Words

SHE SHOT ME DOWN 2305-2

9 titles: Good Thing Going/Hey Look, No
Crying/ Thanks For The Memory/A Long
Night/ Bang Bang/Monday Morning
Quarterback/South To A Warmer Place/I
Loved Her/The Gal That Got Away/It Never
Entered My Mind

L.A. IS MY LADY WPCP3604

11 titles including: L.A. Is My Lady/The Best
Of Everything/How Do You Keep The Music
Playing?/Teach Me Tonight/It's All Right With
Me/Mack The Knife/Until The Real Thing
Comes Along

SINATRA AND SEXTET: LIVE
IN PARIS 45487-2

26 titles including: Goody
Goody/Imagination/At Long Last
Love/Moonlight In Vermont/Without A
Song/Day In, Day Out/I've Got You Under
My Skin/I Get A Kick Out Of You/ The
Second Time Around/Chicago/Nancy

1 9 9 3 –

Back With Capitol Records

DUETS 89611-2 3

13 titles including: The Lady Is A
Tramp/What Now, My Love?/ I've Got A
Crush On You/Summer Wind/ Come Rain Or
Come Shine/New York, New York/They Can't
Take That Away From Me/You Make Me Feel
So Young/ I've Got The World On A
String/Witchcraft

DUETS II 28103-2 2

14 titles including: For Once In My Life/Come
Fly With Me/ Bewitched/The Best Is Yet To
Come/ Moonlight In Vermont/Fly Me To The
Moon/Luck Be A Lady/A Foggy Day/ Where
Or When?/Embraceable You

Picture credits

Archive Photos, New York.
BFI Stills, Posters and Designs, London, with acknowledgement to Columbia Pictures, MGM, Paramount, Twentieth-Century Fox, United Artists, Warner Bros.
Camera Press, London, with acknowledgement to John Bryson, Ray Johnson, Terry O'Neill, Jerry Watson.
Capitol Records.
Anton Corbijn 1993/Capitol Records/Island.
Kobal Collection, London.
London Features International.
Jeffrey Mayer/Pictorial Press, London.
© 1995 Terry O'Neill, pages 136, 140–1, 144.
Don Ornitz.
Pictorial Press, London.
Range/Bettmann/UPI.
© Redferns, London, with acknowledgement to William Gottlieb, David Redfern, Bob Willoughby.
Rex Features, London/Sipa Press, with acknowledgement to Europress, Globe Photos, Peter Martin, Pierluigi (Roma), Phil Roach, Goksin Sipahiogu.
Dennis Stock/Magnum Photos, London, pages 74–5.
© 1995 Bob Willoughby, pages 12, 18, 47, 48, 80, 98, 115, 116, 118–19, 133.
Every reasonable effort has been made to acknowledge the ownership of copyrighted photographs included in this volume. Any errors that may have occurred are inadvertent and will be corrected in subsequent editions, provided notification is sent to the publisher.